W9-AUY-929

CAVALIER

KING CHARLES SPANIEL

FROM THE EDITORS OF
DOG FANCY MAGAZINE

CONTENTS

K9 Expert Education 4
By Allan Reznik, Editor-at-Large, DOG FANCY magazine

The Cavalier Attitude 6
The Cavalier King Charles Spaniel isn't a spoiled royal. He's a trusted, spunky companion dog that loves nothing better than being around his owners.

The Complete Cav 20
Our simple two-page guide gives you all the necessary information about the CKCS — in 300 words or less!

The King of Spaniels 22
England's King Charles II made him popular in the 1600s, but the Cavalier has conquered many countries since. By the 20th century, he was established as a popular American breed, supported by two strong breed clubs.

Choosing a Cav 32
Find out how to choose a reputable breeder and pick a healthy puppy, or maybe you'd like to adopt a dog from a shelter or rescue organization. Either way, there are plenty of Cavs out there waiting for homes.

Home Essentials 44
You need to puppy-proof — or Cav-proof — your house, as well as make sure that you have all the things he requires to be comfortable, such as bedding, toys and lots more.

Housetraining His Highness 58
Your first job is getting your Cavalier to do the doo where you want him to. Using a crate — aka a modern-day den — will expedite the process.

Health for Happiness 70
Selecting a vet means doing some research and planning your Cav's first vet visit. Also, learn what to do when everyday bumps and bruises come about.

Food Fit for a King 86
With proper knowledge and know-how, you can feed your Cav a sound diet so he won't end up a pudgy pooch.

Royal Grooming 98

From nail-clipping instruction to brushing and bathing basics, we'll have your Cavalier King Charles Spaniel looking like royalty.

Training a Toy 110

Every toy dog needs to learn the basic cues of sit, down, stay and come, and additional training advice will make your dog obey without hassle.

Cavs Gone Wild 122

A well-behaved dog isn't born that way. When problems arise, prompt training will turn bad habits into appropriate behavior. Teach your dog that there are better ways to get attention, and you'll save yourself a lot of headaches.

Dog Sports and Activities 136

This toy breed loves to play and be active. You can harness his energy into productive activities like agility, flyball, musical freestyle, conformation and more.

The Golden Years 150

You can't stop Father Time, but you can ease your sweet Cavalier into his senior years.

Resources 162

Index 174

Cavalier King Charles Spaniel, a Smart Owner's Guide®
part of the Kennel Club Books® Interactive Series®
ISBN: 978-1593787-53-0. ©2011

Kennel Club Books Inc., 40 Broad St., Freehold, NJ 07728. Printed in China.

*photographers include Isabelle Francias/BowTie Inc.; Tara Darling/BowTie Inc.;
Gina Cioli and Pamela Hunnicutt/BowTie Inc.; Shutterstock.com*

For CIP information, see page 176.

K9 EXPERT

If you've brought a Cavalier King Charles Spaniel into your home from a responsible breeder or a rescue group — or you are planning to do so — congratulations! You have fallen in love with one of the most appealing breeds in all of dogdom.

Historically, Cavaliers travelled in royal circles. Paintings from the 15th and 16th centuries show the breed with the children of aristocrats, yet today's Cavalier does not require a castle to thrive. He is equally content in the city or the country, strutting down Rodeo Drive or stretched out on a bed of straw, cuddling with seniors or keeping gentle children entertained.

The American Kennel Club breed standard, a written description of an ideal Cavalier King Charles Spaniel, describes the Cavalier as "sporting in character" although he is a member of the Toy Group. Weighing between 13 and 18 pounds, the breed should be sturdy, with moderate bone. Since Charles I (1600–1649) of Britain was the "cavalier king," the dogs were expected to keep up with his horses. Today, Cavaliers love to hike and swim with energetic owners. They'll accompany you cross-country skiing but are just as happy to sit by the fire and snuggle while you read a book.

Looking into the Cavalier's eyes, it's impossible not to smile. The breed standard explains that the "sweet, gentle, melting expression" is a hallmark of the breed. With long, silky ears framing his face, there is no kinder, more loving dog.

Unlike many other glamorous breeds, the Cavalier doesn't need a day at the spa to look his best. His coat is luxurious but of

moderate length; ears, chest, legs and tail are generously feathered, but combing and brushing a few times a week will keep the tangles away.

The Cavalier comes in four colors: Blenheim, tricolor, ruby, and black and tan. The most frequently seen is Blenheim: rich patches of chestnut red on a pearly-white background. The name comes from Blenheim Palace in England, where the Cavalier was originally bred. The dramatic tricolor is a combination of jet-black markings well distributed on the same pearly-white background, with rich tan markings over the eyes, on the cheeks, inside the ears and on the underside of the tail. The ruby is a solid-colored rich red. The black-and-tan coloring is jet black with bright tan markings over the eyes, on the cheeks, inside the ears, and on the chest, legs and underside of the tail. The Blenheims and tris tend to be laidback, while the rubies and black-and-tans are more headstrong.

Cavalier King Charles Spaniels are incredibly social dogs without a mean, dominant bone in their bodies. They will march up to any strange dog they see and expect it to react in the same, friendly manner. Since not all dogs will respond in kind, exercise caution at your local dog park. Be aware, too, that coddling this breed, while easy to do, can result in a needy, clingy Cavalier. Resist the urge to baby your puppy.

If you are the competitive type, Cavaliers can excel in a host of activities from conformation shows to obedience, agility and rally. They bond easily and remain utterly devoted to their owners.

With this Smart Owner's Guide®, you are well on your way to getting your toy dog diploma. But your Cavalier education doesn't end here.

You're invited to join in **Club Cav™** (**DogChannel.com/Club-Cav**), a FREE online site with lots of fun and instructive features such as:

◆ **forums, blogs** and **profiles** where you can connect with other Cavalier owners
◆ **downloadable charts** and **checklists** to help you be a smart and loving toy dog owner
◆ access to Cavalier **e-cards** and **wallpapers**
◆ interactive **games**
◆ canine **quizzes**

The **Smart Owner's Guide** series and **Club Cav** are backed by the experts at DOG FANCY® magazine and DogChannel.com — who have been providing trusted and up-to-date information about dogs and dog people for more than 40 years. Log on and join the club today!

The breed's popularity is understandable. This is a charmer. If you are looking for a sweet and gentle companion, you can't go wrong with a Cavalier King Charles Spaniel.

Allan Reznik
Editor-at-Large, DOG FANCY

ATTITUDE

There are many excellent reasons to choose a Cavalier King Charles Spaniel as your new companion. This breed is affectionate, playful, intelligent and willing to repay an owner's care and attention with complete devotion.

Although considered a lap dog because of his size, the Cavalier is a fearless, sporting little dog. The breed is friendly and nonaggressive, which makes an excellent and adaptable companion for many different homes and lifestyles.

Members of the breed combine their love for people with a sporting personality that, despite their size, makes them avid birders, hunters and hikers. Many Cavalier King Charles Spaniels are just as birdy as larger spaniels, and they point and flush instinctively. They've been known to squeal with frustration when not allowed to chase pigeons on city streets, and many are superb retrievers. Squirrels, mice, butterflies, bugs — anything moving attracts their attention and activates their prey drive.

Did You Know?

Because the Cavalier King Charles Spaniel is so people oriented, they are suited to homes where at least one family member is around most of the day. If that's not possible, you should consider acquiring a pair of Cavaliers so they can keep each other company until their "laps" arrive home from work or school.

PHYSICAL CHARACTERISTICS

Although a small breed, the Cavalier King Charles Spaniel is neither too small nor too delicate. The largest of the Toy Group breeds, the Cavalier weighs on average between 12 to 18 pounds and stands 12 to 13 inches at the shoulders. He's a small, well-balanced dog that can be easily picked up and carried by his owner when necessary. When showing, the breed is easily lifted onto a table for assessment by the judge.

A Cavalier King Charles Spaniel is also a highly suitable breed to carry in a dog crate, something that is especially useful when traveling by car because this safety measure prevents the chance of escape when doors are opened or in case of an accident. In short, the Cavalier is as handsome and portable a companion as anyone could wish for.

Another aspect of Cavalier King Charles Spaniels that owners find endearing is their array of coat colors. Cavalier coat colors include Blenheim (red and white), ruby (all red), black and tan, and tricolor (black and white with tan markings). The Blenheim is the most popular and is generally the

Cavaliers crave company. Aside from humans, they often love other Cavs the best.

easiest to find from a reputable breeder. Ideally, Blenheim and tricolor varieties' markings should be well broken up. Tricolors are black and white with tan markings over the eyes, on the cheeks, inside the ears and legs, as well as on the underside of the tail.

Black and tan can be yet another striking color combination. The black should be what is described as "raven black," and the tan markings should be found above the eyes, on the cheeks, inside the ears, on the chest, on the legs and on the underside of the tail. These tan markings should be bright, but

Cavaliers exist in four main color variations (Blenheim pictured), but they all have the same sweet mug.

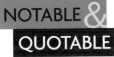

NOTABLE & QUOTABLE

The most fun my family has had with our Cav, Cooper, is watching him play with our other dog, Scully. Even though Scully is three times Cooper's size, Cooper is constantly trying to grab things out of Scully's mouth. Watching them play is hilarious.

— Cav owner Laura Roth-Shofron of Aliso Viejo, Calif.

any white is undesirable. Technically, a Cavalier that is black and tan is described as a "whole color," and any white found in the coat would be incorrect in the show ring.

Rubies are whole-colored in a rich red, and (like black and tans) any white on the coat is undesirable for the show ring. Sometimes a ruby puppy is born with a small fleck of white on the head, but this will usually disappear by 7 or 8 months of age.

Whatever the color of your Cavalier King Charles Spaniel, his coat will require regular grooming. However, compared with some other breeds, the required grooming is not excessive. The Cavalier is quite small and doesn't have as much coat as a Maltese or rough Collie, for example. However, a consistent grooming routine is needed in order to keep the coat from mating and tangling.

PERSONALITY POINTERS

The Cavalier's pleasant and adaptable personality will generally be happy with whatever lifestyle he's offered, and he'll be content with a regular walk around the block, a trip to the dog park or a good energetic game of fetch in your backyard. At other times of day, the Cavalier will be quite content to join his owner watching TV, curled up on the sofa or resting comfortably

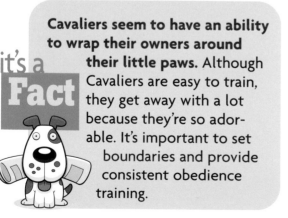

it's a Fact **Cavaliers seem to have an ability to wrap their owners around their little paws.** Although Cavaliers are easy to train, they get away with a lot because they're so adorable. It's important to set boundaries and provide consistent obedience training.

Cavaliers love spending time with their owners — be it for a day at the beach or curled up together on a couch at home.

in a corner of the sitting room. The Cavalier is a breed that is often described as "a people dog," one that appreciates, enjoys and indeed needs human company.

The Cavalier King Charles Spaniel generally gets along well with other dogs and household pets. Of course, when introducing any dog to a new companion, exercise caution. In the case of Cavaliers, such introduction is rarely stressful for any party concerned. Like many other breeds, Cavaliers seem to thoroughly enjoy the company of other dogs, although many owners note that Cavaliers can be a bit snobbish and enjoy the company of other Cavaliers the best.

Many owners like to keep a couple of Cavaliers as pets, as they make for happy companions and are easy to look after. Owning and caring for multiple Cavs does require a little more work than just having one, but it's easily managed. Although no one should regularly leave dogs alone for long periods of time, a Cavalier will usually appreciate the company of a canine companion if his owner has to be away from home for a few hours from time to time.

The Cavalier King Charles Spaniel can be equally at home with a large, boisterous family as he can with a single person, whatever that person's age. Children, however, should always be instructed to handle any dog gently and never to tug on a dog's coat or tail. Children should always be supervised around Cavaliers, especially puppies, for the safety and well-being of the dogs and children. The breed can be happy living with energetic owners who are likely to take their dogs out on long, exciting walks, but they can also live a comfortable and happy life following a more sedentary existence. In either case, a Cavalier King Charles Spaniel will need regular exercise and physical activity.

it's a Fact

Cavaliers love children. Unlike most toy breeds, they're sturdy enough to roughhouse with kids. That said, interactions with younger children should be strictly supervised. A Cav, like any other dog, needs protection from being dropped, stepped on or teased.

My Cavaliers, Ben and Nellie, are loving and great company. They add a lot of joy to our house. They like to sit on my lap and be cuddled, something my children have outgrown. They're good company on a walk, too.

— *Dario DellaMaggiore of Irvine, Calif.*

If you choose to get a Cavalier, you'll soon learn that your dog serves as an ambassador for his species. Even people who are fearful of dogs can come to love a Cavalier.

A Cavalier's rightful place is in your home, included in your family's daily life. In the mind of an adoring dog, one owner is quite sufficient as a family, provided that person gives him all the care and attention he needs and deserves.

There are always exceptions to every rule, but the Cavalier is not usually described as a "yappy" dog. Like most dogs, they'll bark at strangers or unfamiliar noises, but they're not suitable guard dogs because their nature is too soft to deter any intruder.

It's always wise to walk your dog on a leash in unfenced areas. Although Cavs don't have the long legs of breeds like the Whippet or Greyhound, it is surprising how quickly those little legs can move. It's important to remember that your dog's safety is of paramount importance and that a dog on the loose in the wrong place can end in tragedy.

IQ TEST

By normal canine standards, the Cavalier has a fairly high IQ, and many of his senses, such as smell and hearing, are more highly developed than those of humans. Generally speaking, Cavaliers are eager to please their owners, so they do very well learning performance activities like obedience, agility and flyball.

Cavaliers do easily assimilate the fears and joys of their owners, so it follows that a somewhat nervous person may convey that feeling to the dog, who might adapt a rather similar personality. Conversely, a highly boisterous or bubbly person is likely to end up with a Cavalier with a similar personality.

Show your artistic side. Share photos, videos and artwork of your favorite breed on Club Cav. You can also submit jokes, riddles and even poetry about Cavaliers. Browse through the various galleries and see the talent of fellow Cavalier owners. Go to **DogChannel.com/Club-Cav** and click on "Galleries" to get started.

Joy to the World

Elizabeth Joy (Lizzie to her friends), a Blenheim Cavalier King Charles Spaniel owned by Adrienne Escoe of Tustin, Calif., embodies a number of Cavalier traits, good and bad.

"She is extremely affectionate and free with kisses," Escoe says. "She wiggles her butt madly from side to side when she meets someone new, and she licks everyone, especially if they have lotion or sweat on their skin. She is a doggie of extremes. If she is sad or jealous, it shows all over her face. If she is happy, she giggles audibly. If she sees bird feathers in the grass, she goes nuts, jerking madly from one to another. She becomes a maniac with cars, although she is getting better."

When Lizzie sees something she wants, she pulls hard on her leash and barks loudly and constantly; no treat or verbal correction can bring her back to reality.

The good news for Escoe is that this behavior usually diminishes with maturity. The bad news is that emotional maturity may not come for another couple of years. Cavaliers retain puppy-like behaviors well into adulthood and sometimes never entirely give them up. Even the most sedate adult Cavalier will suddenly burst into play, chasing younger dogs around and around the dining room table, down the hall and onto the sofa.

Even a senior Cavalier will pull himself off the couch to chase something of interest.

THE COMPLETE CAV

Get to know the friendliest dog in the neighborhood.

COUNTRY OF ORIGIN: Great Britain

WHAT HIS FRIENDS CALL HIM: King, Prince, Moo, Elvis, Charlie, Chuck, Chuckles, Buddy

SIZE: height — 12 to 13 inches; weight — 13 to 18 pounds

COAT & COLOR: The Cavalier's long, silky coat and dropped ears are defining characteristics. His coat comes in black and tan, ruby (red), Blenheim (white with chestnut markings), and tricolor (black, white and tan).

PERSONALITY TRAITS: Easygoing and loyal, Cavs are a joy to be around. They're friendly and outgoing to most everyone they meet.

WITH KIDS: Cavaliers crave attention; so they thrive in families with plenty of time to devote to them. The perfect lap dog, this gentle and affectionate breed just wants to spend time with his family.

WITH OTHER ANIMALS: Cavs typically play well with others, regardless of species.

ENERGY LEVEL: low to moderate

GROOMING NEEDS: Brush his coat at least two to three times weekly — more often when he sheds. Bathe him and trim his nails at least monthly.

TRAINING ABILITY: easy, intelligent breed

LIVING ENVIRONMENT: This toy breed doesn't need much space, but be sure to take yours on daily walks to let him stretch his legs.

LIFESPAN: 9 to 11 years

The charming Cavalier King Charles Spaniel can trace his ancestors back to small toy spaniels that are found in many paintings from the 16th, 17th and 18th centuries. Such dogs were favorites of the royals and nobles of the day, and because of this, many were depicted with their owners and with children, making for some delightful family portraits. The first portrait in England that depicts the breed is one of Queen Mary I with her husband, Philip of Spain, accompanied by a pair of small spaniels lying at their feet. It was painted in 1554 by Antonio Moro.

The devotion of the Cavalier King Charles Spaniel is legendary. In some accounts, it has been said that a little black and white toy spaniel hid beneath the skirts of Mary Queen of Scots at her execution in 1587. Even after her death, the little dog would not leave his dead mistress.

During Tudor times (1485-1603), these small spaniels were highly popular as ladies' pets, and under the House of Stuart (1603-1714), they were actually given the

Hugh Dalziel wrote in his famous book *British Dogs*, published in 1881: "The Merry Monarch [King Charles II of England] did many more foolish things than take under his royal care and favor, and thereby raising to court, the beautiful toy spaniel which still bears his name."

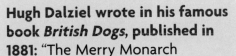

name King Charles Spaniels. King Charles I was accompanied by a small spaniel when he was imprisoned at Carisbrook Castle after the first English Civil War (1642-1646) between the Royalists (known as Cavaliers) and the Parliamentarians (known as Round-heads). Charles was later beheaded after he was defeated during the second civil war (1648–1649), and it is said that his dog Rogue was paraded around the city by a Roundhead, though the fate of the little dog is not known.

The breed's biggest champion, however, was Charles' heir, King Charles II (known as the Merry Monarch), who helped distinguish the breed from other toy spaniels. His extreme devotion to these beautiful and tractable companions is the stuff of legends.

As an adult, Charles kept a pack of spaniels in his bedroom, even allowing female Cavs to whelp puppies in his personal chamber, a practice many members of the household viewed with disdain. He kept many spaniels and probably took the larger, sturdier dogs on his travels by horse and ship. The smaller, more delicate dogs made perfect gifts for ladies of the court.

Charles and his brother, James II, had a pact to continue breeding the toy spaniels, even in the event of Charles' death. James was so committed to the preservation of the dogs that one story tells of a shipwreck in which James was heard yelling, "Save the dogs!" and, as if an afterthought, "... and the Duke of Monmouth!"

The popularity of the King Charles Spaniels seemed to go somewhat out of fashion, especially once King William III and Queen Mary II ascended to power in 1689. The new monarchs preferred Pugs and other short-faced breeds imported from Asia.

Cavaliers endured in and around certain country estates, most notably at Blenheim Palace (home of John Churchill, the first Duke of Marlborough). The Blenheim variety of Cavalier King Charles Spaniel — a white dog with chestnut markings — was favored by the Duke of Marlborough, and one legend explains the origin of the desired lozenge (diamond-shaped) mark on top of the toy spaniel's head.

One evening, when the Lady Marlborough was particularly anxious about her husband, who was away during war, she sat up all night with her favorite female Cavalier, who was about to whelp a litter of puppies. The legend says that, in her anxiety, she continually stroked and pressed on the head of her pet, and when the puppies were born, they all carried her thumbprint on their heads. This mark, called the Blenheim spot, is still desirable in the Blenheim variety of the Cavalier King Charles Spaniel today.

In other parts of England, the toy spaniel evolved over the next few centuries to look more like the Asian breeds favored by William and Mary: shorter face, undershot jaw, domed skull, and larger, protruding eyes. A flatter-faced version evolved to become the English Toy Spaniel (called the King Charles Spaniel in England).

AN AMERICAN IN LONDON

In 1926, a 68-year-old American breeder named Roswell Eldridge went to England and was dismayed to find that the toy

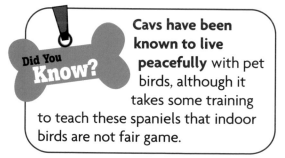

Did You Know?

Cavs have been known to live peacefully with pet birds, although it takes some training to teach these spaniels that indoor birds are not fair game.

NOTABLE & QUOTABLE

From the pictures of early Cavaliers, you can see that some of the structure wasn't quite what it might be now, but some of the dogs in old pictures look like they would be good dogs if you could see them at a better angle. The lovely 'spaniel gentle' seen in pre-Victorian paintings looks much like the breed we know today, perhaps a little lighter-boned with a finer muzzle. This old type was virtually lost when the flat-faced type became popular.

— breeder Joanne Nash of Los Altos Hills, Calif.

spaniels he so admired in the paintings of the old masters had all but disappeared. The fashion of the day was so dramatically in favor of the flatter-faced toy spaniels that spaniels with the "old-fashioned" head were considered incorrect, and any that arose in litters of puppies were never bred.

Eldridge preferred the look of the old toy spaniel. In order to seduce breeders into reviving this old type, he offered a prize of 28 pounds — a good sum of money in those days — at the 1926 Crufts Dog Show in England for the best female and male of the old type, with the Blenheim markings that most closely resembled those in the familiar paintings. His challenge was largely met with disdain, as this style of spaniel was no longer considered correct; yet the prize money — to be awarded at the next five shows — sparked the interest of breeders.

About a month after Eldridge's death in 1928, Miss Mostyn Walker presented a dog called Ann's Son at the Crufts show and was awarded Eldridge's prize. Unfortunately, Eldridge never got to see the dog, but the appearance of this old-style toy spaniel spurred a group of interested fanciers to name the breed the Cavalier King Charles Spaniel and to form a breed club to seek official recognition by England's Kennel Club.

The club wrote a breed standard (a written description of the ideal specimen of a breed) to describe this "new" old breed, based on careful study of Ann's Son and reproductions of many of the paintings picturing toy spaniels from the 16th, 17th

and 18th centuries. The goal of the club was to create, preserve and maintain a natural dog of the old type by breeding to longer-nosed toy spaniels — the very dogs who were considered undesirable because they didn't match the current fashion of flatter-faced spaniels.

Purists claim that only these throwbacks of the older type from English Toy Spaniel litters were used to create and solidify the Cavalier King Charles Spaniel. Some believe that other breeds — such as the English Cocker Spaniel, the Scottish Spaniel and the Papillon — might have been introduced to quickly solidify the Cavalier King Charles Spaniel type, although nobody knows for sure.

In 1945, England's Kennel Club recognized the Cavalier King Charles Spaniel as a separate and distinct breed from the flatter-faced King Charles Spaniel (the breed later known in the United States as the English Toy Spaniel). The Cavalier King Charles Spaniel's career began anew, and in 1970, a few decades after recognition, a virtually unknown Cavalier named Alansmere Aquarius won Best in Show at Crufts before he had even attained a championship title. Since then, the Cavalier King Charles Spaniel continues to be one of the most popular toy breeds in England.

THE UNITED STATES OF CAVALIER

In the 1940s, the Cavalier King Charles Spaniel began to appear in America, but the breed wasn't well known until 1952,

You have an unbreakable bond with your dog, but do you always understand her? Go online and download "Dog Speak," which outlines how dogs communicate. Find out what your Cavalier is saying when she barks, howls or growls. Go to **DogChannel.com/Club-Cav** and click on "Downloads."

Despite their Toy grouping, Cavaliers are considered sporty dogs and often love to chase birds and other animals in nature.

when Sally Lyons Brown received a black-and-tan female puppy named Psyche of Eyeworth as a gift from a friend in England. Brown soon became enamored with the breed, collected more dogs and finally petitioned the American Kennel Club to recognize the breed.

To attain AKC recognition, a breed must have records of multiple generations and an organized club of fanciers to maintain the breed as separate and distinct. The AKC explained to Brown that, although they were interested in officially recogniz-

ing the Cavalier King Charles Spaniel, fanciers must form a club, write a breed standard, hold dog shows, keep track of pedigrees and generate more interest in the breed.

In 1954, Brown founded the Cavalier King Charles Spaniel Club-USA. In 1962, Brown's sister-in-law, Trudy Brown, took over where Sally left off, creating and defining the club. The CKCSC-USA eventually decided not to pursue AKC recognition beyond the breed's status as a member of the Miscellaneous Class, which allowed the Cavalier King Charles Spaniel to compete in obedience trials but not in conformation shows.

In 1992, with the Cavalier King Charles Spaniel a recognized breed in every major country in the world except the United States, the AKC decided to grant the breed full recognition. The AKC invited the club to become the official AKC-recognized parent club — the breed club that represents an AKC-recognized breed at the national level — for the Cavalier King Charles Spaniel.

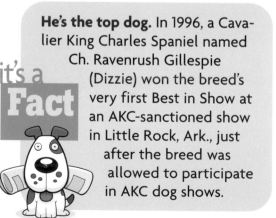

it's a Fact

He's the top dog. In 1996, a Cavalier King Charles Spaniel named Ch. Ravenrush Gillespie (Dizzie) won the breed's very first Best in Show at an AKC-sanctioned show in Little Rock, Ark., just after the breed was allowed to participate in AKC dog shows.

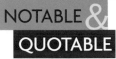
The thing that is amazing about Cavaliers is that they are as wonderful in disposition as they are in looks. Everybody is devoted to their breed, but a beautiful Cavalier with a typical Cavalier personality? There is just no nicer dog on the face of the earth.

— *Barbara Garnett Wilson of Nordland, Wash., a Cavalier breeder and author*

This request deeply divided the club's members. Many of them worried that AKC recognition would result in overbred or commercially bred Cavaliers and would compromise the quality of the breed. Others felt that if the AKC was going to recognize the breed anyway, the Cavalier King Charles Spaniel's future should be guided by experienced and caring stewards of the breed — and who better than devoted members of an already established club?

In the end, the CKCSC-USA, which included a large voting membership, voted not to accept the role as parent club. However 12 members decided to accept the responsibility of forming a parent club.

In 1994, the members formed the American Cavalier King Charles Spaniel Club, the organization that the AKC today formally recognizes as the national parent club of the breed.

Both clubs currently exist, and both register the Cavalier King Charles Spaniel and hold their own dog shows. Many breeders are members of both clubs and register their dogs with both AKC as well as the CKCSC-USA.

Just how quickly will your Cavalier puppy grow? Go to Club Cav and download a growth chart. You also can see your puppy's age in human years. The old standard of multiplying your dog's age by seven isn't quite accurate. Log onto **DogChannel.com/Club-Cav** and click on "Downloads."

JOIN OUR
ONLINE
Club
Cav™

The American Kennel Club officially accepted the Cavalier King Charles Spaniel as a recognized breed in 1995.

CHAPTER 3

CHOOSING

A CAV

The decision to live with a Cavalier King Charles Spaniel is a serious commitment and not one to be taken lightly. A puppy depends on his owner for his entire life. Beyond the basics for survival — food, water, shelter and protection — he needs much, much more. A new pup needs love, nurturing and a proper canine education to mold him into a well-behaved canine citizen. Your Cavalier's health and good manners will need consistent monitoring and regular tuneups, so your job as a responsible dog owner will be ongoing throughout every stage of his life. If you are not prepared to accept these responsibilities and commit to them for the next decade or longer, then you are not prepared to own a dog of any breed.

Although the responsibilities of owning a dog may tax your patience at times, the joy of living with a Cavalier King Charles Spaniel far outweighs the workload, and a well-mannered adult dog is worth your time and effort. Before your very eyes, your new dog will grow up to be your most loyal friend, unconditionally devoted to you.

Once you've found a Cavalier King Charles Spaniel breeder, you can begin the process of choosing a puppy — assuming that the breeder has puppies available. Cavaliers tend to have relatively small litters — generally only three to five puppies.

it's a **Fact**

FINDING THE RIGHT PUPPY

Finding the right puppy for your family is an exciting journey that consists of research, education and locating a responsible Cav breeder. Obtaining a purebred dog should not be an impulse purchase, nor is it a time for bargain shopping. A great place to find a breeder is through the American Kennel Club. Each breed has a national parent club that endeavors to educate breeders and the public about the breed, including health issues and proper care. A parent club is a national organization, but there are also regional clubs affiliated with it throughout the country. This type of breed club is an excellent resource for a list of breeders in your area.

For Cavaliers, the AKC-sanctioned breed club is the American Cavalier King Charles Spaniel Club. Another well-respected breed club with breeder referrals is the Cavalier King Charles Spaniel Club-USA. For more information about these two clubs, see "The United States of Cavalier," starting on page 26.

Responsible breeders will be happy to have you visit their homes to see where and how their puppies are being raised and cared for. Visiting with the puppies and their breeder should be an education in itself. The area where the puppies are being raised should be clean and well maintained. The breeder's puppies themselves should look clean, vigorous and healthy. Depending on the age of the puppies, the breeder should be planning to deworm them and have a plan in place for vaccinations. At a minimum, a reputable Cavalier breeder should:

◆ belong to either a regional or national breed club;
◆ be involved with either conformation, obedience or agility;
◆ raise puppies in a clean environment;
◆ offer a written sales contract that gives a definite period of time to have the puppy's health checked by a veterinarian (this assures the puppy's good health at the time of purchase);
◆ provide written instructions to care for and feed your puppy;
◆ provide a home for the puppy at any point throughout his life if you are no longer able to care for him; and
◆ perform the recommended health tests on the puppy's parents.

If a breeder doesn't meet these criteria, keep looking until you find one who does. Also, be prepared for a reputable breeder to ask you questions about yourself, your home and your family. A good breeder will want to research you as much as you want to research them!

Breed research, breeder selection and puppy visitation are very important aspects of finding the puppy of your dreams. Beyond that, these things also lay the foundation for a successful future with your pup. Puppy personalities vary within each litter, from the shy and easygoing puppy to the one who is dominant and assertive, with most pups falling somewhere in between.

By spending time with the puppies, you will recognize certain behaviors and what these behaviors indicate about each pup's temperament. Which type of pup will complement your family dynamics is best determined by observing the puppies in action with their littermates. The breeder's expertise and recommendations are also valuable. Although you may fall in love with a bold and brassy male, the breeder may suggest another pup that would be best for you. The breeder's experience in rearing Cavalier pups and matching their temperaments with appropriate families offers the best assurance that your pup will

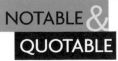
You don't want to buy a puppy from a breeder who avoids contact with you once you've purchased a puppy. You should establish a relationship with each other that lasts for the life of the dog. — Deborah Ayer, a Cavalier breeder from The Plains, Va.

meet your family's needs and expectations. The type of puppy that you select is just as important as your decision that the Cavalier King Charles Spaniel is the breed for you.

BREEDER PAPERS

Everything today comes with an instruction manual. When you purchase a Cavalier, it's no different. A reputable breeder should give you a registration application; a sales contract; a health guarantee; the dog's complete health records; a three-, four- or five-generation pedigree; and some general information on behavior, care, conformation, health and training.

Registration Application. This document from the American Kennel Club or United Kennel Club assigns your puppy a number and identifies the dog by listing his date of birth and the names of the parents, and it shows that he is registered as a purebred Cavalier. It doesn't, however, prove whether or not your dog is a show- or a pet-quality Cavalier and doesn't provide a health guarantee.

Sales Contract. A reputable breeder should discuss with you the terms of the contract before asking you to sign it. This is a written understanding of both of your expectations about the puppy and shows that the breeder cares about the puppy's welfare throughout his life. The contract can include such terms as requiring you to keep the dog indoors at night, spaying or neutering if the puppy isn't going to be a show dog, providing routine veterinary care throughout the dog's life and assuring that you'll feed your dog a healthy diet. Some breeders might ask that you take your dog to obedience classes and earn him a Canine Good Citizen title before he's 2 years of age. Many breeders also require new owners to provide their homes with totally secure fencing and gates around their yards.

Health Guarantee. This includes a letter from a veterinarian that states that the puppy has been examined and is healthy. The guarantee should also show in writing that the breeder will compensate you for the dog if the pup develops a genetic, life-threatening illness during his lifetime.

Health Record. The should have everything you want to know about your puppy's health, as well as his parents'. It should include the dates the puppy was vaccinated, dewormed and examined by a vet for signs of a heart murmur, plus the parents' test results for the presence or absence of hip and elbow dysplasia, cardiac problems and slipped patellas.

Pedigree. The breeder should give you a copy of the puppy's three-, four- or five-generation pedigree. Many breeders

Did You Know?

In 1992, the American Kennel Club approached the Cavalier King Charles Spaniel Club-USA with a request to admit the Cavalier as an AKC-recognized breed, with the CKCSC-USA as the parent club. The membership overwhelmingly voted against the proposal. But a dozen respected breeders who felt AKC recognition was inevitable and not necessarily bad for the breed, worked with the AKC to form a new club, the American Cavalier King Charles Spaniel Club. This became the official AKC parent club for the Cavalier.

Do your homework on the breed before you seriously consider bringing a Cavalier into your home. You want to make sure you find the right fit for your household.

Questions to Expect

Be prepared for the breeder to ask you some questions, too.

1. Have you previously owned a Cavalier King Charles Spaniel?

The breeder is trying to gauge how familiar you are with the Cavalier. If you have never owned one, illustrate your knowledge of the breed by telling the breeder about your research.

2. Do you have children? What are their ages?

Some breeders are wary about selling a puppy to families with younger children. This isn't a steadfast rule, and some breeders only insist on meeting the kids to see how they handle puppies. It all depends on the breeder.

3. How long have you wanted a Cavalier King Charles Spaniel?

This helps a breeder know if your purchase is an impulse buy or a carefully thought-out decision. Buying on impulse is one of the biggest mistakes owners can make. Be patient.

Join Club Cav to get a complete list of questions a breeder should ask you. Click on "Downloads" at **DogChannel. com/Club-Cav**

Early socialization is important for a dog's lifelong interaction with people.

also have photos of the dogs' ancestors that they will proudly share with you.

General Information. The best breeders pride themselves on handing over a notebooks full of the latest information on the Cavalier King Charles Spaniel's behavior, care, conformation, health and training.

it's a Fact

Cavaliers are prone to certain inherited health conditions, including mitral heart disease, hip dysplasia, patellar luxation, cataracts and retinal dysplasia. To prevent the transmission of those conditions to future generations, reputable Cavalier breeders spend the money needed to determine that their breeding dogs are free of them.

Be sure to read it because it will provide invaluable help while you raise your dog.

SOCIALIZATION

The first 20 weeks of your puppy's life are very important. A properly socialized puppy will grow up to be a confident and stable adult who will be a pleasure to live with and a welcome addition to the family.

The importance of socialization cannot be overemphasized. Research on canine behavior has shown that puppies who are not exposed to new sights, sounds, people and animals during their first 20 weeks of life will grow up to be timid and fearful, even aggressive, and unable to flourish outside of their home environments.

Socializing your puppy is not difficult and, in fact, will be fun for you both. Leash training goes hand-in-hand with socialization, so your puppy will be learning how to walk on a lead at the same time that he's

With the popularity of Cavalier King Charles Spaniels, shelters and rescue groups across the country are often inundated with sweet, loving examples of the breed — from the tiniest puppies to senior dogs.

Often, to get the spaniel of your dreams, all it takes is a trip to the local shelter. Or, perhaps you can find your ideal dog waiting patiently in the arms of a foster parent at a nearby rescue group. It just takes a bit of effort, patience and a willingness to find the right dog for your family, rather than just the cutest dog on the block.

The perks of owning a Cavalier King Charles Spaniel are plentiful: companionship, unconditional love, true loyalty and laughter, just to name a few. So why choose the adoption option? Because you will literally be saving a life!

Owners of adopted dogs swear they're more grateful and loving than any dog they've owned before. It's almost as if they knew what dire fate awaited them and are so thankful for the help. Cavaliers, known for their people-pleasing personalities, seem to embody this mentality whole-heartedly when they're rescued. And they want to give something back. Another perk: Almost all adopted dogs come fully vetted, with proper medical treatment, vaccinations and medicine. They're also most likely already spayed or neutered. Some are even licensed and microchipped.

Don't disregard older dogs, thinking your only good pairing will be with a puppy. Adult Cavs are more established behav-iorally and personality-wise, helping to better mesh their characteristics with yours in this game of matchmaking. Puppies are always in high demand, so if you open your options to include adults, you will have a better chance of adopting quickly. Plus, adult dogs are often housetrained, are more calm, are less likely to chew your belong-ings and don't need to be taken out-side in the middle of the night ... five times ... in the pouring rain.

The CKCSC-USA and American CKCS club both offer rescue support information, or you can log on to Petfinder.com. Contact information is listed in the Resources chapter on page 162.

ADOPTING A RESCUED DOG

meeting everyone in the neighborhood. Because the Cavalier is such a terrific breed, your puppy will enjoy being "the new kid on the block."

Make sure that your puppy has received his first and second rounds of vaccinations before you expose him to other dogs or bring him to places that other dogs may frequent. Avoid dog parks and other strange-dog areas until your vet assures you that your puppy is fully immunized and resistant to the diseases that can be passed between canines. Discuss socialization with your veterinarian, as some breeders recommend socializing the puppy even before he has received all of his inoculations, depending on how outgoing the puppy may be.

Once you receive the OK from your vet, take your puppy for short walks to the park and to other dog-friendly places where he will encounter new people, especially children. If your new puppy is not used to being around children, it may take him a while to warm up to them.

Cavaliers that haven't been raised around children definitely recognize that they are different from adults. When introducing a Cavalier pup to children, make sure that you supervise these meetings and that the children do not get too rough or encourage him to play too raucously. An overzealous pup can often nip too hard, frightening the child and overly exciting the puppy. A bad experience in puppyhood can impact a dog for life, so a pup that has a negative experience with a child may grow up to be shy or even aggressive around children.

Take your puppy along on your daily errands. Puppies are natural "people magnets," and most people who see your pup will want to pet him. All of these encounters will help to mold him into a confident adult dog. Likewise, you will soon feel like a confident, responsible dog owner, rightly proud of your handsome Cavalier.

Be especially careful of your puppy's encounters and experiences during the 8- to 10-week-old period, which is also called the "fear period." This is a serious imprinting period, and all contact during this time should be gentle and positive. A frightening or negative event could leave a permanent impression that could affect his future behavior if a similar situation arises.

It's important to spay/neuter your new puppy at an appropriate age to help prevent pet overpopulation.

Breeder Q&A

Here are some questions you should ask a breeder and the answers you want to hear.

Q. How often do you have litters available?

A. You want to hear "once or twice a year" or "occasionally" because a breeder who doesn't have litters that often is probably more concerned with the quality of his or her puppies, rather than with making money.

Q. What kinds of health problems do Cavaliers have?

A. Beware of a breeder who says "none." Every breed has health issues. For CKCS, some genetic health problems include mitral valve disease, syringomyelia, dry eye, cataracts and hip dysplasia.

Get a complete list of questions to ask a Cavalier breeder — and the ideal answers — at Club Cav. Log on to **DogChannel.com/Club-Cav** and click on "Downloads."

NEUTERING/SPAYING

Sterilization procedures (neutering for males/spaying for females) are meant to accomplish several purposes. While the underlying objective is to address the risk of pet overpopulation, there are also some medical and behavioral benefits to the surgeries as well. For females, spaying prior to the first estrus (heat cycle) leads to a marked reduction in the risk of mammary cancer. There also will be no manifestations of "heat" to attract male dogs and no bleeding in the house. For males, it has been linked to the prevention of testicular cancer and a reduction in the risk of prostate problems. In both sexes, it sometimes helps diminish urine marking, roaming and mounting behaviors.

In females, spaying is specifically referred to as an ovariohysterectomy. In this procedure, a midline incision is made in the abdomen, and the entire uterus and both ovaries are surgically removed. While this is an invasive surgical procedure, it usually has few complications because it is typically performed on healthy young animals. However, it is major surgery.

In males, neutering has been traditionally referred to as castration, which involves the surgical removal of both testicles. While this is still a significant surgical procedure, it's not as invasive as the female's surgery.

Neutering/spaying is typically done around 6 months of age at most veterinary hospitals, although techniques have been pioneered to perform the procedures in animals as young as 8 weeks of age. Generally, the surgeries on the very young animals are done for the specific reason of sterilizing them before they go to their new homes. This is done in some shelter hospitals as assurance that the animals definitely won't produce any pups. Otherwise, these organizations must rely on owners to comply with their wishes to have the animals "altered" at a later date — something that doesn't always happen.

Healthy Puppy Signs

Here are a few things you should look for when selecting a puppy from a litter.

1. NOSE: It should be slightly moist to the touch, but there shouldn't be excessive discharge. The puppy should not be sneezing or sniffling persistently.

2. SKIN AND COAT: Your Cav puppy's coat should be soft and shiny, without flakes or excessive shedding. Watch out for patches of missing hair, redness, bumps or sores. The pup should have a pleasant smell. Check for parasites, such as fleas or ticks.

3. BEHAVIOR: A healthy Cavalier King Charles Spaniel puppy may be sleepy, but she should not be lethargic. A healthy pup will be playful at times, not isolated in a corner. You should see occasional bursts of energy and interaction with her littermates. When it's mealtime, a healthy puppy will take an interest in her food.

There are more signs to look for when picking out the perfect Cavalier puppy for your lifestyle. Download the list at **DogChannel.com/Club-Cav**

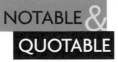

NOTABLE & QUOTABLE

I suggest that puppy buyers 'buy' a breeder first, then wait for the pup. In other words, find someone you like and trust.

— *Christine Solomon, a Cavalier breeder from Long Grove, Ill.*

ESSENTIALS

Adding a Cavalier to your household means adding a new family member who will need your care each and every day for his entire life. When your puppy first comes home, it's important to establish a daily routine with him so that, as he grows up, he'll have a set schedule just as you do. The aspects of your dog's daily care will likewise become regular parts of your day, so you'll both have a new schedule to get used to.

Dogs learn by consistency and thrive on routine. Regular times for meals, exercise, grooming and potty trips are just as important for your dog as they are for you. Your dog's schedule will depend on your family's daily routine, but remember that you now have a new member of the family who is part of your day every day!

Cavalier King Charles Spaniels do have drawbacks, and what's attractive to one person is a turnoff to another. Take the breed's desire to be with people — all the time. Cavaliers follow their people from room to room, back and forth, upstairs and downstairs. It's like having ladies or gentlemen in waiting, and it is perhaps a behavioral echo from the toy spaniels that accompanied their royal masters and mistresses in days gone by.

it's a **Fact**

MEETING THE FAMILY

Your Cavalier's homecoming is an exciting time for all members of the family, and it's only natural that everyone will be eager to meet him, pet him and play with him. However, for your puppy's sake, it's best to make these initial family meetings as uneventful as possible so that your pup isn't overwhelmed with too much too soon.

He has just left his mother and littermates and is away from the breeder's home for the first time. Despite his fuzzy wagging tail, he's still apprehensive and wondering where he is and who all these strange humans are. It's best to let him explore on his own and meet the family members as he feels comfortable. Let him investigate all the new smells, sights and sounds at his own pace. Children should be especially careful not to get overly excited, use loud voices or hug the pup too tightly. Be calm, gentle and affectionate, and be ready to reassure him if he appears frightened or uneasy.

Be sure to show your puppy his crate during this first day home. Toss a treat or two inside the crate; if he associates the crate with food, he will associate the crate with good things. Leave the door ajar so he can wander in and out as he chooses.

FIRST NIGHT IN HIS NEW HOME

So much happens in a puppy's first day away from the breeder. He's had his first car ride to his new home. He's met his new human family and perhaps the other family pets. He's explored his new house and yard, at least those places where he is allowed to be during his first weeks at home. He may have visited his new veterinarian. He has eaten his first meal or two away from his

Did You Know?

Cats and Cavs often live together amicably or at least respectfully. Once your pup knows the cat is in charge, they will often play chase, then curl up on the same sofa. Cavs that aren't familiar with cats as housemates may chase them unless corrected by their owners or the cats. Take the same precautions you would with any other dog when introducing cats and Cavaliers.

Your new puppy will love exploring her new surroundings. Supervise her at all times to make sure she doesn't get into anything dangerous.

mother and littermates. Surely that's enough to tire a 10-week-old Cavalier pup … or so you hope!

Now, it's bedtime. During the day, your pup investigated his crate, which is his new den and sleeping space, so it's not entirely strange to him. Line the crate with a soft towel or blanket that he can snuggle into and gently place him into the crate for the night. Some breeders send home a piece of bedding that the pup slept in with his littermates, and those familiar scents will be a great comfort for him on his first night without his siblings.

He will probably whine or cry. Your puppy is objecting to the confinement and the fact that he is alone for the first time. This can be a stressful time for you and for your pup. It's important that you remain strong and don't let your puppy out of his crate to comfort him. He will fall asleep eventually. If you release him, your puppy will learn that crying results in you letting him out, and he'll continue the habit. You are laying the groundwork for future habits. Some breeders find that soft music can soothe a crying pup and help him get to sleep. There are also stuffed animals that simulate the heartbeat and warmth of a puppy's littermates, which may help your new pup make the transition to being on his own.

LEADER OF YOUR PUPPY'S PACK

Like other canines, your puppy needs an authority figure, someone he can look up to and regard as the pack leader. His first pack leader was his mother, who taught him to be polite and not to chew too hard on her ears or nip at her muzzle. He learned those same lessons from his littermates. If he played too rough, they cried in pain and stopped the game, which sent an important message to the rowdy puppy.

As puppies play together, they are also struggling to determine who'll be the boss.

Make sure you've stocked up on all the essential products before you bring your new puppy home. That includes grooming and entertainment needs, too.

Before you bring your Cavalier home, make sure you don't have anything that can put her in harm's way. Go to Club Cav and download a list of poisonous plants and foods to avoid. Log on to **DogChannel.com/Club-Cav** and click on "Downloads."

As pack animals, dogs need someone to be in charge. If a litter of puppies remained together beyond puppyhood, one of the pups would emerge as the strongest — the alpha, the one who calls the shots.

Once your puppy leaves the pack, he will intuitively look for a new leader. If he doesn't recognize you as that leader, he'll try to assume that position for himself. Of course, it's difficult to imagine your adorable Cavalier puppy trying to be in charge when he is so small and seemingly helpless. You must remember that these are natural canine instincts. Don't cave in and allow your pup to get the upper paw!

Just as socialization is so important during the first 20 weeks, so too is your puppy's early education. He was born without any bad habits. He doesn't know what's good or bad behavior. If he does things like nipping and digging, it's because he is having fun and doesn't know that humans consider these things as bad. It's your job to teach him proper puppy manners, and this is the best time to accomplish that; before he has developed bad habits. It is much more difficult to correct unacceptable behavior than to teach good behavior from the start.

Make sure that all members of the family understand the importance of being consistent when training the new puppy. If you tell your puppy to stay off the sofa and your child allows him to cuddle on the couch to watch television, your pup will be confused about what he is and is not allowed to do. Have a family meeting before your pup comes home so everyone understands the basic principles of puppy training, understands the rules you have set forth for your pup and agrees to follow them.

The old saying that "an ounce of prevention is worth a pound of cure" is especially true when it comes to puppies. It is much easier to prevent inappropriate behavior than it is to change it. It's also easier and less stressful for your pup, since it'll keep discipline to a minimum and create a more positive learning environment for him. It will also be easier on you!

Here are a few tips to keep your belongings safe and your puppy out of trouble:

◆ Keep your closet doors closed and your shoes, socks and other apparel off the floor so your puppy can't get at them.

◆ Keep a secure lid on the trash container or put the trash where your puppy can't dig into it. He can't damage what he can't reach!

◆ Supervise your puppy at all times to make sure he isn't getting into mischief. If he starts to chew the rug, distract him by tossing a toy for him to fetch. You also will be

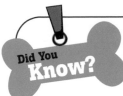

When the Cavalier genome is unraveled, scientists will be sure to find a gene for lap sitting. Cavaliers epitomize the term "lap dog" — in a good way. Like furry, heat-seeking missiles, they search out and establish themselves in any available lap, whether it belongs to their person or to someone they've just met. For most Cavaliers, no one is a stranger, simply a new best friend.

When your lap isn't available, your Cav will happily find alternative lounging places. So provide her with a pet bed if you don't want dog hair all over your stuff.

able to whisk him outside when you notice that he is about to have an accident. If you can't see your puppy, you can't teach or correct his behavior.

YOUR CAVALIER SHOPPING LIST

Just as expectant parents prepare a nursery for their baby, so should you ready your home for the arrival of your Cavalier pup. Purchase the necessary supplies and have them in place before he comes home, to ease the transition from the warmth and familiarity of his mother and littermates to the brand-new environment of his new home and human family. You will be too busy to stock up and prepare your house after your pup comes home, that's for sure! Imagine how a pup must feel upon being transported to a strange new place. It's up to you to comfort your little pup and to let him know that he's going to be happy in his new home!

Food and Water Bowls: Your puppy will need separate bowls for his food and water. Stainless steel is generally preferred over plastic bowls since stainless steel is sterile and pups are less inclined to chew on the metal. Heavy-duty ceramic bowls are popular, but consider how often you'll have to pick up those heavy bowls! Buy adult-sized pans; your puppy will grow into them before you know it.

Crate: If you thought that crates are tools of punishment and confinement for when a dog has misbehaved, think again. Most breeders and almost all trainers recommend a crate as the preferred housetraining tool, as well as for all-around puppy training and safety. Because dogs are natural den creatures and prefer cave-like environments, there are many benefits to crate use. The crate provides your puppy with his very own "safe house," a cozy place to sleep, take a break or seek comfort with a favorite toy; a travel aid to house your dog when on the road, at hotels or at the vet's office; a training aid to help teach your puppy proper elimination habits; and a place of solitude when dog-phobic people happen to drop by.

Crates come in several types, although wire and fiberglass crates are most popular. Both are safe, and your puppy will adjust to either one, so the choice is up to you. The wire crates offer better visibility for your pup, as well as better ventilation. Many of the wire crates easily collapse into easy-to-transport sizes. The fiberglass crates, similar to those used by the airlines for animal transport, are sturdier and more den-like. However, the fiberglass crates don't collapse and are less ventilated than wire ones, which can be problematic in hot weather. Some newer crates are made of heavy plastic mesh; they are very lightweight and are also collapsible. However, a mesh crate might not be suitable for a pup with manic chewing habits.

Don't bother with a puppy-sized crate. Although your Cavalier will be a wee little fellow when you bring him home, he will grow in the blink of an eye, and your puppy crate will be useless before you know it.

NOTABLE & QUOTABLE

My Cavalier, Bentley, possesses the breed standard characteristics, plus a certain intuition that defies definition. I have seen him act differently with different people, depending on what their needs were. He seems to have a sixth sense, which maybe other dogs understand, but I certainly don't. I just stand back and watch him in awe. — Diane Zdrodowski of Blairstown, N.J., cofounder of Canine Assisted Resources in Education and owner of a CKCS therapy dog

Purchase a crate that will accommodate an adult Cavalier. He will stand about 12 to 13 inches when full grown, so a medium-sized crate will fit him nicely.

Bedding and Crate Pads: Your puppy will enjoy some type of soft bedding in his crate, something he can snuggle into to feel cozy and secure. Old towels or blankets are good choices for a young pup, since he may (and probably will) have a housetraining accident or two in the crate or decide to chew on the material. Once he is fully housetrained and out of the early chewing stage, you can replace your puppy bedding with a permanent crate pad. Crate pads and other dog beds run the gamut from inexpensive to high-end designer styles, but don't splurge on the good stuff until you are sure that your puppy is reliably housetrained.

Toys: Just as infants and older children require objects to stimulate their minds and bodies, puppies need toys to entertain their curious brains, wiggly paws and achy teeth. A fun array of safe toys will help satisfy your puppy's chewing instincts and distract him from gnawing on the leg of your antique chair or your new leather sofa. Most puppy toys are cute and look as though they would be a lot of fun, but not all are necessarily safe for your pup, so be sure to use caution when you go out shopping for dog toys.

Although Cavaliers are not known to be as voracious chewers as many other breeds, they still love to chew. The best "*chew-cifiers*" are nylon and hard rubber bones, which are safe to gnaw on and come in sizes appropriate for all age groups and breeds. Never give your Cavalier a cooked natural bone, which can splinter or develop dangerous sharp edges; pups can easily swallow or choke on bone splinters. In addition to being a choking hazard, these sharp pieces can damage your dog's intestinal tract; veterinarians often tell of surgical nightmares involving bits of splintered bone.

Rawhide chews, while a favorite of most dogs and puppies, can be equally dangerous. After they become soft from chewing, pieces of rawhide can be easily swallowed, and dogs have been known to choke on them. Rawhide chews should be offered only when you can supervise your puppy.

Soft or plush toys are special favorites. They come in a wide variety of cute shapes and sizes, and some look like little stuffed animals. Puppies love to shake them up and toss them about or simply carry them around. Beware of fuzzy toys that have small eyes or

noses that your pup could chew off and swallow, and make sure that he doesn't disembowel a squeaky toy to remove the squeaker!

Braided rope toys are similar in that they are fun to chew and toss around, but they shred easily, and the strings are easy to swallow. The strings are not digestible, and your puppy could end up at the vet's office if he doesn't pass them in his stool. As with rawhides, closely monitor your puppy when he plays with rope and plush toys. If you believe that your pup has ingested any of these objects, call your veterinarian right away. You might have to check your dog's stools for the next couple of days to see if he passes them. At the same time, also watch for signs of intestinal distress.

A simple all-time favorite toy for dogs (young and old) is an empty plastic gallon jug for milk (or juice or water, etc.). Such containers make lots of noise when they are batted about, and puppies go crazy with delight as they play with them. However, they don't last very long, so be sure to remove and replace them when the ends get chewed to shreds.

NOTABLE & QUOTABLE

When my husband had bilateral knee surgery, he had to stay in bed for six weeks and our dogs stuck completely by his side. They were used to going out every day and getting a chance to run in the park, but that seemed to be the least of their worries. They were going to be there with him.

— Cav owner Tamela Klisura of Mission Viejo, Calif.

Collars: A lightweight nylon collar is the best choice for a young pup. Quick-clip collars are easy to put on and remove, and you can easily adjust them as your puppy grows. Introduce him to his collar as soon as he comes home, to get him accustomed to wearing it. Make sure that it's snug enough that it won't slip off, yet loose enough to be comfortable for your pup. You should be able to slip two fingers between the collar and your dog's neck. Check the collar often, as puppies grow in spurts and his collar can become too tight almost overnight.

Leashes: A 6-foot nylon leash is an excellent choice for a young puppy. It's lightweight and not as tempting to chew on as a leather one. You can switch to a 6-foot leather lead after your pup has grown and is used to walking politely on a leash. You don't want him wandering too far away from you at first, and you'll want to keep him in his potty area when taking him out for house-training purposes.

Once your puppy can heel with a 6-foot leash, you can consider purchasing one in a retractable style. This type of lead allows your dog to roam farther away from you and explore a wider area when you're out walking, and it also retracts when you need to keep him close to you.

HOME SAFETY FOR YOUR PUPPY

The importance of puppy-proofing cannot be overstated. In addition to making your house comfortable for your Cavalier's arrival, you also must make sure that your house is safe for your puppy before you bring him home. There are countless hazards in the owner's personal living environment that a pup can sniff, chew, swallow or destroy. Many are obvious; others are not. Do a thorough house check before bringing your puppy home to remove or rearrange any-thing that could hurt him, keeping any potentially dangerous items out of areas he has access to.

Electrical cords are especially dangerous, since puppies view them as irresistible chew toys. Unplug and remove all exposed cords or fasten them beneath a baseboard where your puppy cannot reach them. Veterinarians and firefighters can tell you horror stories about electrical burns and house fires that resulted from puppy-chewed electrical cords. Protecting your puppy from cords is essential for his safety and the safety for the rest of your family.

Scout your home for tiny objects that might be seen at a pup's level. Keep medication bottles and cleaning supplies well out of reach, and do the same with waste baskets and other trash containers. Never use rodent poison or other toxic chemicals, and keep these containers safely locked up. You will be amazed at how many places a curious puppy can discover!

Once your house has cleared inspection, check your yard. A sturdy fence, well embedded into the ground, will give your dog a safe place to play and potty. Although Cavaliers aren't known to be climbers or jumpers, they are still athletic dogs, so a 5- to 6-foot-high fence should be adequate to contain an agile youngster or adult. Check the fence periodically for necessary repairs. If there is a weak link or a space to squeeze through, you can be sure that a determined Cavalier will discover it.

The garage and shed can also be hazardous places for a pup, as things like fertilizers, chemicals and tools are usually kept there. It's best to keep these areas off-limits. Antifreeze is especially dangerous to dogs, as they find the taste appealing and it takes only a few licks from the driveway to kill a dog of any size.

Get down to your Cavaliers' eye level while dog-proofing your home. If something is within their reach, you can bet they're going to inspect it.

HIS HIGHNESS

There's a big difference between training an adult dog and training a young puppy. With a young puppy, *everything* is new! At 8 to 10 weeks of age, he'll be experiencing many things, and he has nothing with which to compare these experiences. Up to this point, he has been with his mother and littermates, not one-on-one with people except in his interactions with his breeder and visitors to the litter.

When you first bring your puppy home, he is eager to please you. This means that he accepts doing things your way. His development during the next couple of months will a lay foundation for most everything he needs to know for the rest of his life. After that, for the next 18 months, it's up to you to reinforce good manners by building on the foundation you've established. Once your puppy behaves reliably in response to basic cues and has reached the appropriate age, you may gradually introduce him to some of the interesting sports, games and activities available to pet owners and their dogs.

Having a canine shadow doesn't bother everyone, but some people find it annoying. It can also be a problem if a Cavalier must be left alone frequently. Cavaliers can develop separation anxiety if they don't get the human interaction and attention they crave.

it's a **Fact**

Raising your puppy is a family affair. Each member of the family must know what rules to set for your puppy and how to use the same cues to mean the same things every time. Even if your family is large, your pup will soon consider one person as the leader — the alpha in his pack, the "boss" who must be obeyed. Often that highly-regarded person is the one who feeds the puppy. Food ranks very high on the puppy's list of important things! That's why you will reward your puppy with small treats and verbal praise when he responds correctly. As the puppy learns to do what you want, gradually eliminate food rewards and just continue to use

praise. If you were to continue giving food treats, you could have two problems on your hands: an obese dog and a beggar.

Training begins the minute your Cav puppy steps through the doorway of your home, so don't make the mistake of just letting him explore on his own when you first bring him home. It tells him to "Go for it! Run wild!" Instead, gently but firmly show your puppy that you are the boss. An uncertain pup may be terrified to move, while a bold one will be ready to take you at your word and start plotting to destroy the house!

When you first arrive home, take your new puppy directly to his potty area. After the car ride home, there's a good chance your puppy will need a potty break. Instead of gambling to have an accident inside the house, see if you can get him to use the new outside potty area. Don't worry if he doesn't use the area right away. It will take time for your new puppy to adjust to his new surroundings, but your gentle attention will quickly make him comfortable in his new home.

ADULT DOGS

If you've adopted an adult dog who is already housetrained, lucky you! You're off the hook! However, if the dog has spent most of his life in a kennel or in a home that lacked any real training, be prepared to tackle the job ahead. A dog 3 years or older with no previous training can't be blamed for not knowing something he was never taught. While the dog is trying to understand and learn your rules, he also has to unlearn many of his previous habits and his overall view of the world.

Working with a professional trainer will speed up your progress with an adopted adult dog. You'll need patience, too. Some

Most dogs don't figure out the whole housetraining thing right away. Repetition and consistency are crucial to helping a dog learn what's expected, and time is necessary for her to develop the physical capacity to "hold it" between trips outside. Once your dog has been accident-free for a month or so, and if she's at least 6 months old, you can consider her housetrained.

new rules may be nearly impossible for a dog to accept. After all, so far he's successfully done everything his own way! He may agree with your instruction for a few days and then slip back into his old ways, so you must be just as consistent and understanding in your teaching as you would be with a puppy. Your dog will have to learn to pay attention to your voice, your family, the daily routine, new smells, new sounds and, in some cases, even a new climate.

It's extremely important to learn how a newly adopted adult dog reacts to meeting children (yours and others), strangers, your friends and other dogs. If he wasn't socialized with dogs as a puppy, this could be a major problem. This doesn't mean he's a bad or aggressive dog; rather, it just means he has no idea how to read another dog's body language. There's no way for him to tell whether the other dog is a friend or foe, so he may act aggressively. This behavior calls for professional help; even then, you may not be able to correct the behavior. If you have a puppy, it's important to introduce him properly to other puppies and friendly adult dogs.

CRATETRAINING

Cratetraining your puppy is important for many reasons. It's one of the most effective ways to housetrain a new puppy. Also, a puppy that is in his crate while his owner is away from home will not destroy any furniture and will be safe from any household hazards. A dog that is comfortable in a crate can be safely transported in a car or airplane and makes a great hotel guest. So, for a new puppy, cratetraining and housetraining essentially happen at the same time.

One of the biggest mistakes new owners commonly make is giving their puppies too much freedom when they first arrive in their new homes.

First, find an area that will become your puppy's living space. For many people, this spot is in or near the kitchen because the floor cleans up easily. This space needs to be near a busy family area to acclimate your pup to a variety of noises — everything from pots and pans to the telephone, blender and dishwasher.

This living area should be a safe place for your puppy, where you can leave him for a few minutes at a time unsupervised. You may also need to purchase baby gates or an exercise pen (aka an X-pen) in order to enclose the room you've chosen. Keep a crate in this area, too. Many people mistakenly think that crates are used for punishment; nothing could be further from the truth. In fact, you want to make his time in the crate a very positive experience.

Remember: It's important to set up the rules and routines that you want your puppy to follow from the very beginning. You can always give your puppy more freedom as he grows and matures, but it's more difficult to take away freedom. Your puppy will strenuously object with a lot of whining and barking!

Most times when a dog isn't housetrained, it is the human who has the problem. What I believe gives small dogs the bad reputation is that people are less likely to work as hard on housetraining a little dog because cleaning up the problem isn't huge — literally — as is the case with a larger dog, and because of the cuteness factor, which leads people to spoil and coddle their smaller dogs.

— Cathy Brown, a rescue volunteer from New Castle, Pa.

If your Cavalier King Charles Spaniel puppy repeatedly has the same accident in the same place, you need to do a better job of cleaning up her accidents. Be sure to use a cleaner formulated especially for pet stains — bypass club soda, ammonia or any other all-purpose products. Enzyme-based animal-product cleaners will work the best.

Puppies have a built-in instinct that makes them want to avoid soiling their own dens or sleeping areas. Therefore, your puppy won't want to eliminate in his crate. Essentially, cratetraining uses your dog's instinct to help housetrain him. This is why it's best to have your new puppy sleep in his crate at night and stay in it when you are unable to closely supervise him. He won't want to soil his crate.

The crate must only be large enough for your puppy to stand in and turn around. You don't want him to be able to eliminate at one end of the crate and sleep at the

When you first arrive home from the breeder, take your new puppy to his approved potty spot before stepping inside your house.

Having problems housetraining your Cavalier? Ask other Cavalier King Charles Spaniel owners for advice and tips, or post your own success story to give other owners encouragement. Log onto **DogChannel.com/Club-Cav** and click on "Community."

Successful housetraining requires: scrupulous management, constant supervision, appropriate use of leashes, crates and tethers, and regular trips to the outdoor bathroom spot — every hour on the hour, at first.

Other regular housetraining tips to use: Feed regular meals instead of free-choice feeding, remove water before bedtime and switch to a different kind of crate substrate, if necessary.

other. If you have an adult-sized crate for your Cavalier pup, you should purchase (or create) a divider to make the space inside the crate smaller. As your dog grows or is reliably housetrained, you can make the space bigger.

Placing toys and treats in the crate goes a long way toward getting your puppy to accept the crate as his home. Safe toys in the pup's crate or enclosed area will keep him occupied, but monitor their condition closely. Discard any toys that show signs of excessive chewing. Squeaky parts, bits of plastic or stuffing, or any other small pieces can cause intestinal blockage or possibly choking if they're swallowed. Most Cavaliers become

Cavalier King Charles Spaniels are a clean and intelligent breed, so housetraining shouldn't be an issue.

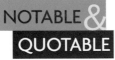
It all goes back to socialization. The more things puppies are exposed to in a positive manner while young, the better equipped they'll be to handle new situations.
— *Caryl Wolff, a certified dog trainer in Los Angeles, Calif.*

accustomed to their crates and actually grow fond of them, seeking them out as places to sleep long after they are adults. There may be one or two mishaps along the way, but, by and large, your dog's instinct will be to keep his crate free of waste.

Although the crate is a wonderful training tool, don't confine your puppy for long periods of time during the day. As a general rule, a puppy can only hold his waste for the same number of hours that he is months old. In other words, a 4-month-old Cavalier should not be left alone during the day longer than four consecutive hours without an opportunity for a potty break.

It's important to keep your puppy on a consistent schedule during housetraining. As soon as you get up in the morning, take him out of the crate and directly outside to the area you want him to use for elimination. Puppies will need to go potty first thing in the morning, shortly after they eat, directly after play periods and after waking up from a nap.

When you take your puppy outside to relieve himself, use a short cue such as "outside" or "Go potty." Accompany your puppy outdoors every time and praise him lavishly for eliminating in the appropriate spot. Remember that puppies don't always know they need to go potty until a second before they go. Housetraining takes patience. To prevent accidents, it's important to watch for signs that your puppy

needs to go, such as pacing, whining, circling and sniffing. Any time you see these behaviors, take your puppy outside immediately. When you can't closely watch your puppy for these signs or can't take him outside at least every hour, you should confine him to his crate.

If you catch your puppy in the act of eliminating inside the house, make a loud noise to interrupt his action and immediately take him outside. If you don't catch your puppy in the act, don't punish or scold him because he won't understand what action he's being scolded for. Never rub your puppy's nose in his waste; it's not an effective training method. If your puppy does have an accident inside the house, use an enzyme-cleaning solution to eliminate the odor of dog elimination as soon as possible. Regular household cleaners won't do the trick. Invest in the largest container of pet deodorizer you can find. Puppies are attracted to eliminate in places by smell; if they sniff out a spot that's been used before they'll take that as a sign to use it again. So you must thoroughly clean up after your puppy with an appropriate product.

Housetraining can be a long process that will take up a lot of your time, so be patient. Your Cavalier will eventually figure out what you want. Dogs don't have accidents in the house to be spiteful or uncooperative. Puppies have small bladders, and they just can't hold their urine for very

Did You Know?

When you start housetraining, take your dog to the potty spot: when she wakes up in the morning, after a nap, after she eats and after she plays. For puppies younger than 4 months of age or for a very tiny housetrainee, this can mean 12 to 14 trips to the potty place daily. Older puppies may get by with six to 10 trips; adult dogs should get three to five bathroom breaks each day.

long. If your Cavalier puppy is having a lot of accidents inside the house, make sure you take him outside at least every hour during the day. If it's still an issue, you may want to take your him to the vet; ongoing housetraining difficulties may be caused by an underlying health concern.

SMART TIP!

Be consistent. Scheduling meals and bathroom breaks at the same time every day will give your canine housetrainee the structure she needs to learn to regulate her urge to eliminate.

HAPPINESS

As your Cavalier's owner, you become his default health advocate. This means that it's up to you to make sure that he visits the veterinarian regularly and that you monitor his health throughout his life. Your veterinarian will be your partner in your dog's times of good health and bad. Together, you will make minor and major decisions about your Cavalier's health.

FIRST STEP: SELECT THE RIGHT VET

The selection of a veterinarian for your dog should be based on personal recommendations of the doctor's skills, and, if possible, his experience with Cavalier King Charles Spaniels. If the veterinarian is based nearby, it will be helpful and more convenient because you might have an emergency or might need to make multiple visits for treatments.

All licensed veterinarians should be capable of dealing with routine medical issues such as infections and injuries, as well as the promotion of good health (like vaccinations). If the problem affecting your

> **Did You Know?**
>
> **The American Cavalier King Charles Spaniel Club is taking an active, aggressive role** in raising funds to support research in the health issues that affect Cavaliers by directly funding their own research studies, as well as cofunding studies with the AKC Canine Health Foundation.

spaniel is more complex, your vet may refer you to someone with more detailed knowledge of what is wrong. This usually will be a specialist such as a veterinary dermatologist or a veterinary ophthalmologist.

Veterinary procedures are costly and are going to become more expensive as treatments improve. It is acceptable to discuss matters of cost with your vet; if there is more than one treatment option, cost may be a factor in deciding which route to take.

Smart owners will look for a vet before they actually need one. For newbie pet owners, start looking for a veterinarian a month or two before you bring home your new Cavalier puppy. That will give you time to meet candidate veterinarians, check out the condition of the clinic, meet the staff and decide who you feel most comfortable with. If you already have a spaniel puppy, look sooner rather than later, preferably not in the midst of a veterinary health crisis.

FIRST VET VISIT

It is much easier, less costly and more effective to practice preventive medicine than to fight bouts of illness and disease. Properly bred puppies of all breeds come from parents who were selected based upon their genetic disease profiles. The puppies' mother should have been vaccinated, free of all internal and external parasites and properly nourished. For these reasons, a visit to the veterinarian who cared for the mother is recommended if at all possible. The mother passes disease resistance to her puppies, which should last from 8 to 10 weeks. Unfortunately, she can also pass on parasites and infection. This is why knowing about her health is useful in learning more about the health of her puppies.

Once you have your Cavalier puppy home safe and sound, it's time to arrange for his first trip to the veterinarian. Perhaps the breeder can recommend someone in the area who specializes in Cavaliers, or maybe you know other Cavalier owners who can suggest a good vet. Either way, you should make an appointment within a couple of days of bringing your puppy home. If possible, see if you can stop for this first vet appointment before going home.

The pup's first vet visit will consist of an overall examination to make sure that your pup doesn't have any problems that aren't apparent to you. The veterinarian also will set up a schedule for the pup's vaccinations; the breeder should inform you of which ones your puppy has already received, and the vet can continue from there.

Your puppy also will have his teeth examined and have his skeletal conformation and general health checked prior to certification by the veterinarian. Puppies in certain breeds have problems with their kneecaps, cataracts and other eye problems, heart murmurs and undescended testicles. They may also have behavioral problems, which your veterinarian can evaluate if he or she has had the relevant training.

Picking the right vet is one of the most important decisions you'll make for the lifelong health of your new family member. Make sure you ask the right questions to ensure that your vet is knowledgeable not only about dogs but also about Cavalier King Charles Spaniels in particular. Download a list of questions to ask potential vets by logging on to **DogChannel.com/Club-Cav.** Click on "Downloads."

JOIN OUR
ONLINE
Club
Cav™

Take your Cavalier for regular vet checkups to keep her in shape for an active lifestyle.

VACCINATION SCHEDULING

Most vaccinations are given by injection and should only be given by a veterinarian. Both you and the veterinarian should keep a record of the date of the injection, the identification of the vaccine and the amount given. Some vets give a first vaccination at 8 weeks of age, but most dog breeders prefer the course not to commence until about 10 weeks because of interaction with the antibodies produced by the mother. The vaccination scheduling is usually based on a 15-day cycle. You must take your veterinarian's advice as to when to vaccinate, as this may differ according to the vaccine used.

The usual vaccines contain immunizing doses of several different viruses such as distemper, parvovirus, parainfluenza and hepatitis. There are other vaccines available when the puppy is at a greater risk of viral exposures. You should rely on your veterinarian's advice. This is especially true for the booster immunizations. Most vaccination programs require a booster when the puppy is a year old and once a year thereafter. In some cases, circumstances may require more frequent immunizations.

Kennel cough, more formally known as tracheobronchitis, is combatted with a vaccine that is sprayed into the dog's nostrils. Kennel cough is usually included in routine vaccinations, but it often is not as effective as the vaccines for other major diseases.

Your vet probably will recommend that your Cav puppy be fully vaccinated before you take him on outings. There are airborne diseases, parasite eggs in the grass and unexpected visits from other dogs that might be dangerous to your puppy's health. Other dogs are the most harmful reservoir of pathogenic organisms, as everything they have can be transmitted to your puppy.

6 Months to 1 Year of Age: Unless you intend to breed or show your dog, neuter or spay your Cavalier at 6 months of age. Discuss the procedure with your veterinarian. Neutering and spaying have proven to be beneficial to male and female puppies, respectively. Besides eliminating the possibility of pregnancy, it inhibits (but does not prevent) breast cancer in females dogs and prostate cancer in males.

Your veterinarian should provide your Cavalier puppy with a thorough dental evaluation at 6 months of age, which will ascertain whether all his permanent teeth have grown in properly. Initiate a home dental care regimen by the time your pup is 6 months old. This should include brushing his teeth weekly and providing him with good dental devices (such as nylon bones). Regular dental care promotes healthy teeth, fresh breath and a longer life.

it's a **Fact**

Patellar luxation, or a slipped kneecap, is a common canine orthopedic problem. The disease is seen often in small breeds, including Cavaliers. The disorder is caused by abnormalities in the patella (or kneecap) a flat, movable bone at the front of the knee. It slides up and down in a groove in the femur (the human equivalent of the thigh bone), thus allowing the dog to bend or straighten her leg. The patellar ligament and the attached muscles maintain the patella in its position in this groove.

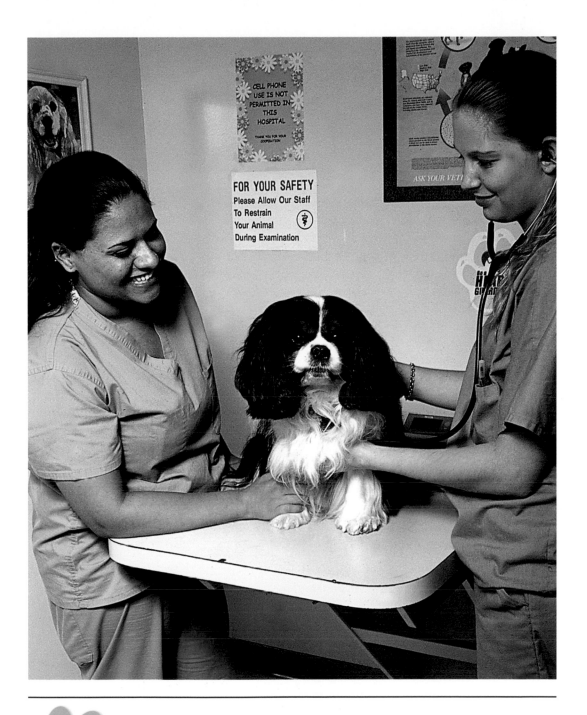

Just like with infants, puppies need a series of vaccinations to ensure that they stay healthy during their first year of life. Download a vaccination chart from **DogChannel.com/Club-Cav** that you can fill out for your Cavalier King Charles Spaniel.

JOIN OUR ONLINE Club Cav™

Dogs Older Than 1 Year: Proper dietary changes recommended by your veterinarian can make life more pleasant for your aging Cavalier and you. Continue to visit the veterinarian at least once a year as bodily functions change with age. A dog's eyes and ears will loose efficiency; and his liver, kidney and intestinal functions often decline.

EVERYDAY HAPPENINGS

Keeping your Cavalier healthy is a matter of keen observation and quick action when necessary. Knowing what's normal for your dog will help you recognize signs of trouble before they blossom into a full-blown emergency situation.

Even if the problem is minor, such as a cut or scrape, you should care for it immediately to prevent infection, as well as to ensure that your dog doesn't make the problem area worse by chewing or scratching at it. Here is what to do for common, minor injuries or illnesses, as well as how to recognize and deal with emergencies.

Cuts and Scrapes: For a cut or scrape that's half an inch or smaller, clean the wound with saline solution or warm water and use tweezers to remove any splinters or other debris. Apply an antibiotic ointment. No bandage is necessary unless the wound is on a paw, which can pick up dirt when your dog walks on it. Deep cuts with lots of bleeding or those caused by glass or some other object should only be treated by your veterinarian.

Cold Symptoms: Dogs don't actually get colds, but they can get illnesses with similar symptoms, such as coughing, runny noses or sneezing. Dogs cough for any number of reasons, from respiratory infections to inhaled irritants to congestive heart failure. Take your Cavalier to the veterinarian for prolonged coughing or coughing accompanied by labored breathing, runny eyes and nose or bloody phlegm.

A runny nose that continues for more than several hours requires veterinary attention, as well. If your Cavalier sneezes, he may

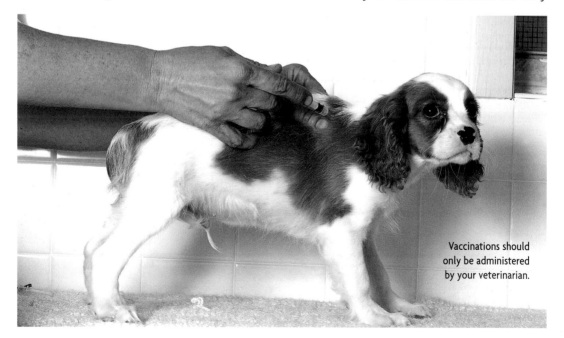

Vaccinations should only be administered by your veterinarian.

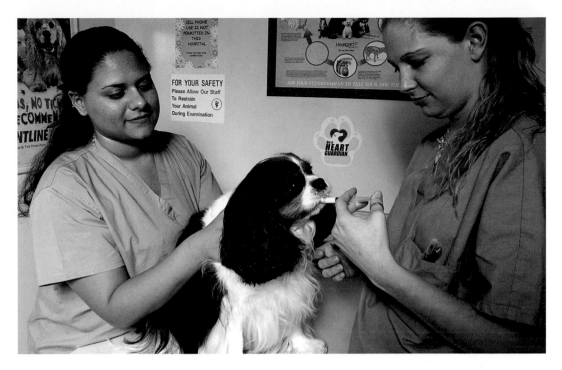

have some mild nasal irritation that will resolve on its own, but frequent sneezing, especially if it's accompanied by a runny nose, may indicate anything from allergies to an infection or something stuck in his nose.

Vomiting and Diarrhea: Sometimes dogs can suffer minor gastric upset when they eat a new type of food, eat too much, eat the contents of the trash bin or become excited or anxious. Give an adult Cavalier's stomach a rest by withholding food for 12 hours, and then feeding him a bland diet such as baby food or unflavored rice and chicken, gradually returning your dog to his normal food. Projectile vomiting or vomiting or diarrhea that continues for more than 48 hours, is another matter. If this happens, immediately take your Cavalier to the veterinarian.

Clogged Anal Glands: A Cavalier's anal glands can cause problems if not periodically evacuated. In the wild, dogs regularly clear their anal glands to mark their territory. In domestic dogs, this function is no longer necessary; thus, their contents can build up and clog, causing discomfort. Signs that the anal glands (located on both sides of the anus) need emptying are if a Cavalier drags his rear end along the ground or keeps turning around to lick the area of discomfort.

While care must be taken not to cause injury, anal glands can be evacuated by pressing gently on either side of the anal opening and by using a piece of cotton or a tissue to collect the foul-smelling matter. If the anal glands are allowed to become impacted, abscesses can form, causing pain and the need for veterinary attention.

Ingesting Poison: Cavaliers can get into all sorts of mischief, so it's not uncommon for them to swallow something poisonous in the course of their investigations. Obviously, an urgent visit to the vet is required under such circumstances. If possible, when you call your vet, inform him which poisonous substance your dog ingested because different treatments are needed for different poisons.

Should it be necessary to cause your Cavalier to vomit (which is not always the case with poisoning), a small lump of baking soda, given orally, will have an immediate effect. Alternatively, a small teaspoon of salt or mustard, dissolved in water, will have a similar effect but may be more difficult to administer and take longer to work.

HEALTH CONSIDERATIONS

Many dogs, whatever their breed, suffer from health issues at some time during their lives, but undoubtedly some breeds seem more prone to certain problems than others. It is important as a dog owner to be well-informed about the health issues that your Cavalier might face during his lifetime. This knowledge will help you monitor your dog's overall health and know what problems to look for.

Mitral valve disease: Mitral valve disease, better known as MVD, is a common heart disease found in Cavaliers. MVD can affect Cavaliers both young and old. The disease, believed to be genetic, affects the mitral valve of a dog's heart. This valve is responsible for correct blood flow from the atria to the ventricles. Vets can identify potential MVD issues by listening to the dog's heartbeat through a stethoscope. A murmur indicates a leak in the dog's heart valve. The presence of a murmur usually indicates that a Cavalier does have some form of MVD.

At this time, it is not possible to determine how this disease will progress once a murmur has been detected. Vets can use X-rays, electrocardiograms and ultrasounds to determine the severity of the disease if a murmur is detected. Sometimes a Cavalier can live a long, happy life with a murmur and otherwise be asymptomatic for the disease. Sadly others can progress rapidly into congestive heart failure. Affected dogs tire easily, breathe rapidly and develop a cough; fainting occurs in severe cases. Vets attempt to slow down the progress of the disease with medication that can offer months or years of life to your Cavalier before he succumbs to congestive heart failure. Responsible breeders will have all their breeding stock checked regularly for MVD. However, because of the genetic complexity of this disease, a dog from two healthy, heart-clear parents can still develop the disease.

Syringomyelia: Syringomyelia is a progressive neurological disease. A malformation in the occipital bone at the base of the skull impedes the normal flow of cerebrospinal fluid causing damage to the spinal cord. Symptoms of SM include: scratching the neck and shoulder area without making contact, unexplained yelping or pain, neck pain or a neck tilt. These symptoms will usually present themselves before the age of 3, but they can appear in a dog's later years as well. Currently, the only way to accurately diagnose SM is with a magnetic resonance imaging test. A qualified neurologist can identify this condition with an MRI and suggest a course of action, which may include medication or surgery. There are other physical issues that include these symptoms, which is why an MRI is necessary for an accurate diagnosis.

Dry eye: Dry eye occurs when normal tear production is impaired. While this condition can be successfully treated with the long-term application of special eye ointments, if left untreated it can cause corneal ulceration and blindness.

Cataracts: Opaque spots in the lens of the eye, cataracts are opacities that can look cloudy on the surface of the eye, even though the cloudy lens is actually deep

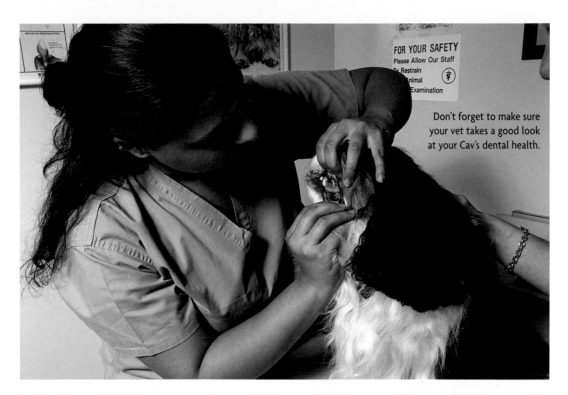

Don't forget to make sure your vet takes a good look at your Cav's dental health.

inside the eyeball. Surgery may be needed to remove the cataract.

Hip dysplasia: Hip dysplasia is a degeneration of the hip joints. HD can affect a dog at any time throughout his life; however, a simple X-ray can diagnose this condition as early as 16 weeks of age. This is a hereditary condition, so a breeder should have the mother and father's hips checked before breeding them.

OTHER HEALTH CONCERNS

Airborne allergies: Just as humans suffer from hay fever during allergy season, many dogs suffer from the same. When the pollen count is high, your Cav might suffer, but don't expect him to sneeze or have a runny nose like a human. Cavaliers react to pollen allergies in the same way they react to fleas; they scratch and bite themselves. Dogs, like humans, can be tested for allergens. Be sure to discuss allergy testing with your vet.

Autoimmune illness: Autoimmune illnesses make a dog's immune system overact and not recognize parts of the affected person. Instead, the immune system starts to react as if these parts were foreign cells that need to be destroyed. An example of an autoimmune illness is rheumatoid arthritis, which occurs when the body does not recognize the joints. This leads to a very painful and damaging reaction in the joints. Rheumatoid arthritis has nothing to do with age, so it can also occur in puppies. The wear-and-tear type of arthritis that affects older people and animals is called osteoarthritis.

EXTERNAL PARASITES

Insect bites itch, erupt and can become infected. Dogs have the same reaction to fleas, ticks and mites. When an insect lands on you, you can whisk it away. Unfortunately, when your Cavalier is bitten by a flea, tick or mite, he can only scratch or bite.

By the time your Cavalier has been bitten, the parasite has done its damage. It may have laid eggs, which will cause further problems. The itching from parasite bites is probably due to the saliva injected into the site when the parasite sucks the dog's blood.

Fleas: Of all the health and grooming problems to which canines are susceptible, none is better known and more frustrating than fleas. Flea infestation is relatively simple to cure but difficult to prevent.

To control flea infestation, you have to understand the flea's lifecycle. Fleas are often thought of as a summertime problem, but centrally heated homes have made fleas a year-round problem. The most effective method of flea control is a two-stage approach: kill the adult fleas, then control the development of pupae (pre-adult) fleas. Unfortunately, no single active ingredient is effective against all stages of the flea lifecycle.

Treating fleas should be a two-pronged attack. First, the environment needs to be treated; this includes carpets and furniture, especially your Cav's bedding and areas underneath furniture. Treat the environment with a household spray containing an insect growth regulator and an insecticide to kill the adult fleas.

Most insecticides are effective against eggs and larvae; they actually mimic the fleas' own hormones and stop the eggs and larvae from developing into adult fleas. There are currently no treatments available to attack the pupae stage of the lifecycle, so the adult insecticide is used to kill the newly hatched adult fleas before they find a host. Most insect-growth regulators are active for many months, while adult insecticides are only active for a few days.

When treating fleas with a household spray, vacuum before applying the product. This stimulates as many pupae as possible to hatch into adult fleas. Also treat the vacuum cleaner with an insecticide to prevent the eggs and larvae that have been collected in the vacuum bag from hatching.

The second treatment stage is to apply an adult insecticide to your Cavalier. Traditionally, this would be in the form of a collar or a spray. Recent innovations include digestible insecticides that poison the fleas when they ingest the dog's blood. Alternatively, there are drops that, when placed on the back of the dog's neck, spread throughout the hair and skin to kill adult fleas.

Ticks: Though not as common as fleas, ticks are found all over the tropical and temperate world. They don't bite like fleas; they harpoon. They dig their sharp proboscis (nose) into the dog's skin and drink the blood, which is their only food. Ticks are controlled the same way fleas are controlled.

The American dog tick, *Dermacentor variabilis*, may be the most common dog tick in many areas, especially those areas where the climate is hot and humid. Most dog ticks have life expectancies of a week to 6 months, depending on climatic conditions. They can neither jump nor fly, but they can crawl slowly.

Did You Know?

About one-third of Cavaliers have macrothrombocytosis (unusually large blood platelets) or asymptomatic thrombocytopenia (unusually low platelet count), which are relatively harmless conditions seen only in this breed.

Because your dog regularly spends time outside, she'll need ongoing flea, tick and mite treatments.

No matter how careful you are with your precious Cavalier King Charles Spaniel, sometimes unexpected injuries happen. Be prepared for an emergency by creating a canine first-aid kit. Find out what essentials you need on **DogChannel.com/Club-Cav** — just click on "Downloads."

Do your part to keep your dog healthy, as well. Practice good health prevention such as heartworm protection, flea and tick protection, vaccinations, good nutrition, regular exercise, weight control and regular veterinary exams. If you notice any changes in your dog's behavior, call your veterinarian: Problems that are diagnosed and treated early often offer a better prognosis than an unchecked problem that results in permanent or more extensive damage.

Mites: Just as fleas and ticks can be problematic for your dog, mites can also lead to itchy fits. Microscopic in size, mites are related to ticks and generally take up permanent residence on their host animals — in this case, a Cav. The term "mange" refers to any infestation caused by one of the mighty mites, of which there are six varieties.

INTERNAL PARASITES

Most animals — fish, birds and mammals, including dogs and humans — have worms and other parasites that live inside their bodies. According to Dr. Herbert R. Axelrod, a fish pathologist, there are two kinds of parasites: smart and dumb ones. The smart parasites live in peaceful cooperation with their hosts — a symbiotic relationship — while the dumb parasites kill their hosts. Most worm infections are relatively easy to control. If they are not controlled, they weaken the host dogs to the point that other medical problems occur, but they do not kill their hosts as dumb parasites would.

Roundworms: These parasites live in the dog's intestines and continually shed eggs. It has been estimated that a dog produces more than 6 ounces of feces every day; each ounce averages hundreds of thousands of roundworm eggs. There are no known areas where dogs often roam that do not contain roundworm eggs. Roundworms can infect people, too, so be sure to have your dog regularly tested for their presence.

Roundworm infection can kill puppies and cause severe problems in adult dogs, as the hatched larvae travel to the lungs and trachea through the bloodstream. Cleanliness is the best prevention. Always pick up after your dog and dispose of his feces in appropriate receptacles.

Hookworms: Hookworms are dangerous to humans, as well as to dogs and cats, and they can cause severe iron-deficiency anemia. The worm uses its teeth to attach itself to the dog's intestines and changes the site of its attachment about six times per day. Each time the worm repositions itself, the dog loses blood and can become anemic. Symptoms of hookworm infection include dark stools, weight loss, general weakness, pale coloration and anemia, as well as possible skin problems. Fortunately, hookworms are easily purged with a number of medications that have proven effective. Discuss these with your veterinarian. Most heartworm preventatives include a hookworm insecticide.

Humans can be infected by hookworms through exposure to contaminated feces. Because the worms cannot complete their lifecycle in a human, the worms simply infest the skin and cause irritation. As a preventative, use disposable gloves or a poop scoop to pick up your Cavalier's droppings and prevent your dog (or neighborhood pets) from defecating in children's play areas.

[Luxation] problems can be noticed any time from when a puppy first tries to walk, up until full growth at about 1 year. The most common time an abnormality is noticed is when the puppy is about half-grown, about 4 to 6 months.

— Jonathan N. Chambers, D.V.M., a professor
of orthopedic surgery at the University of Georgia in Athens

Tapeworms: There are many species of tapeworms, all of which are carried by fleas. Fleas are so small that your Cav could unknowingly pass the tapeworms onto your hands, your plate or your food, making it possible for you to ingest a flea that is carrying tapeworm eggs. While a tapeworm infection is not life threatening in dogs (it's a smart parasite!), if transmitted to humans, it can be the cause of a serious liver disease.

Whipworms: In North America, whipworms are counted among the most common parasitic worms in dogs. Affected dogs may only experience upset tummies, colic and diarrhea. These worms, however, can live for months or years in the dog, beginning their larval stage in the small intestine, spending their adult lives in the large intestine and finally passing infective eggs through the dog's feces. The only way to detect whipworms is through a fecal examination, though this is not always foolproof. Treatment for whipworms is tricky, due to the worms' unusual lifecycle, and often dogs are reinfected due to exposure to infective eggs on the ground. Cleaning up droppings in your backyard and in public places is necessary for sanitary purposes and the health of your dog and others.

Threadworms: Though less common than roundworms and hookworms, threadworms concern dog owners in the southwestern United States and the Gulf Coast area where the climate is hot and humid, which is the prime environment for threadworms. Living in the small intestine of the dog, this worm measures a mere 2 millimeters and is round in shape. Like the whipworm, the threadworm's lifecycle is very complex, and the eggs and larvae are transported through the feces.

A deadly disease in humans, threadworms readily infect people, mostly through the handling of feces. Threadworms are most often seen in young puppies. The most common symptoms include bloody diarrhea and pneumonia. Infected puppies must be promptly isolated and treated to prevent spreading the threadworms to other dogs and humans; vets recommend a follow-up treatment one month later.

Heartworms: These thin, extended worms measure up to 12 inches long and live in a dog's heart and inhabit the major blood vessels around it. Dogs may have up to 200 heartworms. Symptoms may be loss of energy, loss of appetite, coughing, the development of a pot belly and anemia.

Heartworms are transmitted by mosquitoes, which drink the blood of infected dogs and take in larvae with the blood. The larvae, (called microfilariae) develop within the body of the mosquito and are then

Your dog can contract many parasites while outdoors, so have her regularly tested by a vet.

passed on to the next dog bitten after the larvae mature. It takes two to three weeks for the larvae to develop to the infective stage within the body of the mosquito. Dogs are usually treated at about 6 weeks of age and are maintained on a prophylactic dose given monthly to regulate proliferation.

Although this is a dangerous disease, it is difficult for a dog to be infected. Discuss the various preventatives with your veterinarian, because there are many different types now available. Together, you can decide on a safe course of prevention for your Cavalier.

Building a good relationship with your dog's primary caretaker will benefit your Cavalier in many ways.

NOTABLE & QUOTABLE

Many veterinarians are unaware that large platelets occur in Cavaliers. This can lead a veterinarian to misdiagnose the dog. Because genuine thrombocytopenia can be a life-threatening condition, veterinarians noting low blood-platelet counts are often anxious to start treatment, which can create serious problems in a dog with pseudo-thrombocytopenia. Unless a Cavalier has other symptoms besides a low platelet count, treatment is rarely, if ever, advisable.
— Joanne Nash of Los Altos Hills, Calif., Health Committee chairperson
of the American Cavalier King Charles Spaniel Club

FOOD FIT FOR

Feeding your Cavalier King Charles Spaniel the best diet is based on various factors, including age, activity level, overall condition and size. When you visit the breeder, he or she will share with you some advice about the proper diet for your dog based on experience with the breed and the foods with which he or she has had success. Likewise, your vet will be a helpful source of advice throughout the dog's life and can aid you in planning a diet for optimal canine health.

CHOOSING THE BEST FOOD

When selecting the type of food to feed your Cavalier, check the ingredients label. The main ingredient will be listed first on the label; the other ingredients are listed in descending order according to how much is in the food. Many dry-food products have soybean, corn or rice as the main ingredient. While these types are fine, look into dry foods with a meat or fish base. These are better-quality foods and thus higher priced. However, they may be just

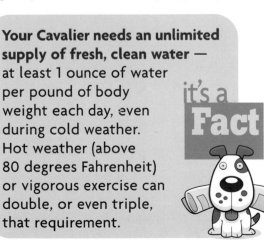

Your Cavalier needs an unlimited supply of fresh, clean water — at least 1 ounce of water per pound of body weight each day, even during cold weather. Hot weather (above 80 degrees Fahrenheit) or vigorous exercise can double, or even triple, that requirement.

it's a
Fact

as economical in the long run because studies have shown that it takes less of the higher-quality foods to maintain a dog's health. So look for a dry dog food that lists a protein source like chicken, turkey, salmon or beef as the first ingredient. Some dog owners avoid foods that contain wheat because some dogs are allergic to it.

WET OR DRY FOOD

In comparing the various types of food — dry, semimoist and canned — dry foods contain the least amount of water, and canned foods have the most. Proportionately, dry foods are the most calorie- and nutrient-dense, which means that you need more of a canned food product to supply the same amount of nutrition. Also, manufacturers have begun to tailor dry dog food to breed size — smaller bites for smaller breeds. Choosing a dog food that works for both you and your dog comes down to personal preference. You may need to try a couple different brands to find one that your Cavalier loves. Water is important for all dogs, but even more so for those fed dry foods because of the low water content.

There are strict controls that regulate the nutritional content of dog food, and in order to be considered "complete and balanced," a food has to meet minimum requirements. It is important that you choose such a food for your dog, so check the label to be sure that you are getting the best-quality food that you can afford. If not, look for a food that clearly states on the label that it is formulated to be complete and balanced for your dog's particular stage of life, whether it be puppy, adult or senior.

Recommendations for how much to feed your Cavalier King Charles Spaniel will also be indicated on the label. Ask your veterinarian about proper food portions, and keep an eye on your dog's weight to see whether the recommended amounts are adequate. If the dog becomes over- or underweight, you will need to make adjustments; this also would be a good time to consult your veterinarian.

The food label may also make feeding suggestions, such as whether moistening a dry product is recommended. Sometimes a splash of water will make the food more palatable for your Cavalier, and it might even enhance the flavor. Don't be overwhelmed by the many factors that go into feeding your dog. Manufacturers of complete and balanced foods make it easy, and once you find the right food and amounts for your Cavalier, his daily feeding will be a matter of routine.

FEEDING YOUR PUPPY

Your puppy's very first food will be his mother's milk. There may be special situations in which pups fail to nurse, necessitating that the breeder hand-feed them with a formula, but for the most part, pups spend the first weeks nursing from their mom. The breeder will wean the pups by gradually introducing solid foods and decreasing nursing. Puppies may even start the weaning process themselves, albeit inadvertently, if they snatch bites from their mom's food bowl. By the time

NOTABLE &
QUOTABLE

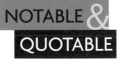

The major dog-food companies spend millions of dollars doing research, and I don't second-guess them. I select a product and stick with it for years. My dogs never know the difference, and unless the manufacturer changes the ingredients, it's likely my dogs will eat the same product all of their adult lives.

— Barbara Hill, a Cavalier breeder from Omaha, Neb., who feeds her dogs dry food mixed with just a bit of canned food (1 tablespoon of canned food per cup of dry food)

the puppies are ready for new homes, they are fully weaned and eating a good puppy food. As a new owner, you may be thinking, "Great! The breeder has taken care of the hard part." But not so fast.

A puppy's first year of life is the time when most of his growth and development takes place. This is a delicate time, and diet plays a huge role in proper skeletal and muscular formation. Improper diet and exercise habits can lead to damaging problems that will compromise your dog's health and movement for his entire life. That being said, new owners should not worry, manufacturers offer a wide variety of dog foods formulated for growing pups.

Since growth-formulated foods are made to provide the nutrition that a growing puppy needs, it is unnecessary and, in fact, can prove harmful to add supplements. Research has shown that too much of certain vitamins and minerals predispose a dog to skeletal problems. This is by no means a case of "if a little is good, a lot is better." At every stage of your dog's life, too much or too little of any nutrients can be harmful, which is why a food labeled "complete and balanced" is the easiest way to know that your dog is getting the proper nutrition he needs.

Young pups have small bodies and accordingly small digestive systems, so divide your Cav's daily portions into small meals throughout the day. This can mean starting off with three or more meals a day and decreasing the number of meals as he matures. Eventually, you can feed only one meal a day, although dividing it into two meals may be healthier for your dog's digestion.

The breeder you purchase your puppy from should provide you with a copy of your pup's current eating schedule and a small supply of the food he's been eating. If you decide to use a different food from what the breeder gave you, make the change gradually to avoid an upset stomach. Start by mixing a small bit of the new food in with the old brand; slowly increase the amount of the new food and decrease the old food until the change is complete.

Feeding your pup at the same times and in the same place each day is important, both for housetraining purposes and for establishing your dog's everyday routine. As for how much to feed, growing puppies generally need proportionately more food per body weight than their adult counterparts, but a pup should never be allowed to become overweight. Dogs of all ages should be kept in proper body condition; extra weight can strain a pup's developing frame, causing skeletal problems.

Did You Know?

Your Cavalier King Charles Spaniel needs proteins, carbohydrates, fats, vitamins and minerals for optimal growth and health. Proteins are used for the growth and repair of muscles, bones and other body tissues. They're also used to produce antibodies, enzymes and hormones. Carbohydrates are metabolized into glucose, the body's principal energy source. Fats are used for energy when glucose is unavailable and are important for hormone production, nervous system function and vitamin absorption. Vitamins and minerals participate in muscle and nerve function, bone growth, healing, metabolism and fluid balance.

Don't change your new puppy's food right off the bat. If you want to feed your Cav something other than what she's used to, start gradual. Mix some new food with the old each day until she's eventually only eating the new stuff.

Watch your pup's weight as he grows and, if the recommended amounts seem to be too much or too little for your pup, consult the vet about appropriate dietary changes. Keep in mind that treats, although small, can quickly add up throughout the day, contributing unnecessary calories. Treats are fine when used prudently; opt for dog treats specially formulated to be healthy or for nutritious snacks like small pieces of cheese or cooked chicken.

FEEDING THE ADULT DOG

For your adult dog, feeding properly is about maintenance, not growth. Again, correct weight is a concern. Your dog should appear fit and should have an evident waist. His ribs should not be protruding (a sign of being underweight), they should be covered by only a slight layer of fat. Under normal circumstances, an adult dog can be maintained fairly easily with a high-quality, nutritionally complete adult-formula food.

Factor treats into your dog's overall daily caloric intake, and never give him table scraps. Overweight dogs are more prone to health problems. Research has even shown that obesity takes years off a dog's life. With that in mind, resist the urge to overfeed and overtreat. Most Cavaliers love to eat, and you must resist those big brown eyes looking up at you for more food. The best way to spoil your Cav is with extra attention, not extra food.

The amount of food needed for proper maintenance will vary depending on your Cavalier's activity level, but you can tell whether the daily portions are keeping him in good shape. With the wide variety of good complete foods available, choosing what to feed is largely a matter of personal preference. Just as with a puppy, give your adult Cavalier a consistent feeding place and mealtimes. In addition to a consistent routine, regular mealtimes also allow the owner to gauge how much his dog is eating. If your dog never seems to be satisfied or becomes uninterested in his food, you'll know right away that something is wrong and can consult your veterinarian.

Occasional treats are fine, but factor them in to your dog's daily caloric intake and subtract a portion of his dinner that night.

If you primarily give your dog dry food, make sure she also drinks plenty of water to stay hydrated. Wet food provides additional water intake that you must make up for when she devours her kibble.

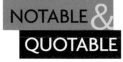

Preventing a weight problem is a lot easier than treating one. Feed your Cavalier scheduled meals, instead of simply allowing her to eat as much as she wants whenever she chooses. Limit between-meal treats (veggies are good low-calorie choices). The owner is in charge of the food bowl. Cavaliers don't make themselves fat, because they are not the ones who fill the food bowl. Plan your dog's snacks as part of his daily food intake so that he doesn't become tubby.
— *Kris Hassig, a Cavalier breeder from Minnetonka, Minn.*

Just like you, your dog needs extra water on hot days, especially when she's just a puppy!

SPECIAL FEEDING CONSIDERATIONS

Active Dogs: The more a dog does, the more he needs to eat! If your Cavalier participates in agility, tracking, obedience or even hunting activities, he may require larger portions of maintenance food than a less active counterpart. You may want to ask your vet about specially formulated "performance" diets for active dogs.

When feeding an active dog, it is essential to provide adequate periods of rest before and after eating to avoid stomach upset or the more serious gastric torsion, which can be fatal. You can also feed treats during rest periods to keep your dog's energy high in between meals, and remember to offer him plenty of water. Your Cavalier needs time to settle down before and after any eating or drinking, so factor breaks into his training program or work routine.

Senior Dogs: On average, once a dog has reached 75 percent of his expected lifespan, he has reached "senior citizen" or geriatric status. Your Cavalier will be considered a senior at about 7 years of age; based on his size, he has a projected lifespan of about 9 to 11 years. (The smallest breeds

Most Cavaliers chow down with nary a problem, except possibly a bit of disappointment when they finish and there isn't anything else to eat. A few unlucky ones finish eating, only to be sabotaged a short time later by vomiting, diarrhea or flatulence. What's the problem? It could be a food sensitivity or intolerance, a localized digestive tract reaction to a food ingredient.

An effective treatment for a food sensitivity is to identify the triggering ingredient by means of an elimination diet, then remove that ingredient from your Cav's diet entirely. This procedure, conducted under the guidance of a vet, is usually reserved for serious sensitivity cases.

If your Cav experiences digestive tract upset only occasionally, you may not need to use an elimination diet, but you should still consult your vet to rule out potentially serious problems. If your Cav checks out all right, you can try to manage the sensitivity with the following strategies (with your vet's approval):

Choose the right food. Feed a nutritionally balanced commercial dog food, unless your veterinarian recommends a prescription diet or homemade food. You might need to try several different products to find one that doesn't cause problems. Once you find the food, make it your Cavalier's sole diet.

Don't feed table food treats. If you simply can't resist giving your Cav an occasional treat, offer small chunks of veggies, which usually cause fewer reactions than high-protein products, such as meat or cheese.

Feed several meals a day. Some dogs have fewer problems if they're fed smaller, more frequent meals. Try three small meals instead of two larger ones.

Avoid the trigger ingredient. If you discover your Cavalier has a problem food, avoid all forms of it. Check the ingredient lists of all edible products, including chewable medication, such as heartworm preventive.

Consult your veterinarian. If these strategies aren't effective or the symptoms increase in frequency or severity, consider an elimination diet to identify the problem ingredient(s).

An important note: Consult your veterinarian immediately if your Cav persistently vomits or has diarrhea; passes blood or mucus in her stool; or seems lethargic, depressed or feverish. The problem could be something more serious than a food sensitivity.

generally enjoy the longest lives, and the largest breeds have the shortest.)

What does aging have to do with your dog's diet? No, he won't get a discount at the local diner's early-bird special. Yes, he will require some dietary changes to accommodate the changes that come along with increased age. One change is that the older dog's dietary needs become more similar to that of a puppy. Specifically, dogs can metabolize more protein as youngsters and seniors than in the adult-maintenance stage. Discuss with your vet whether you need to switch to a higher-protein or senior-formulated food or whether your current adult-dog food contains sufficient nutrition for a senior.

Watching your dog's weight is always essential, even more so in the senior stage. Older dogs are already more vulnerable to illness, and obesity only contributes to their susceptibility to problems. As an older dog becomes less active and exercises less, his regular portions may cause him to gain weight. At this point, you may consider decreasing his daily food intake or switching to a reduced-calorie food. As with other changes, consult your vet for advice before taking action. For more information on senior care, see Chapter 12.

DON'T FORGET THE WATER!

Regardless of what type of food your dog eats, he needs plenty of water. Have fresh, cold water available to your dog in a clean bowl at all times. There are special circumstances (such as during housetraining, when you will want to monitor your pup's water intake to be able to predict when he will need to relieve himself), but water must be available to him nonetheless. Water is essential for a dog's hydration and proper body function.

In the heat or if exercising vigorously, your dog will be more thirsty and will drink more. However, if he begins to drink noticeably more water for no apparent reason, this could signal any of various problems, and you should consult your vet.

Some Cav owners are tempted to give milk from time to time to moisten dry food, but dogs do not have the enzymes necessary to digest the lactose in milk, which is much different from the milk that nursing puppies receive. Therefore stick with fresh water to quench your dog's thirst.

Be a good provider and make sure your Cav gets the proper nutrition she needs.

Most dogs, like most people, love to snack. Those tasty tidbits are so much more fun to eat than plain old everyday food. It's OK to give your Cavalier an occasional treat, as long as you make healthy choices for your canine friend.

When choosing commercial dog treats, check the package label for the nutritional analysis, ingredient list and manufacturer's recommended amount. Some products are actually formulated to provide complete nutrition (of course, they shouldn't be your Cavalier's principal diet). Crunchy treats often have less sugar than soft, moist ones and provide Cavalier-satisfying chewing exercise — features that promote dental health and weight control.

For low-cost alternatives to store-bought snacks, look in your kitchen for the following:

Vegetables: carrots, broccoli stems, green beans, peas; veggies can be cooked, raw or even frozen.

Fruits: apples, pears, bananas; feed in small amounts only and avoid the skin to avoid digestive upsets.

Breads, crackers, dry cereal and other snack foods: unsweetened, low-fat, whole-grain products

Meat treats: Small chunks of cooked lean meat, meatballs of canned dog food; some owners bake liver or slices of canned dog food.

NOTE: Some food products that are safe for humans can be dangerous for dogs. Don't feed your Cavalier chocolate, onions, garlic, grapes, raisins or macadamia nuts — they've all been associated with toxic reactions ranging from vomiting and diarrhea to death.

Finally, if you like to cook, you can make your own Cavalier goodies using recipes specifically formulated for dogs.

GROOMING

A grooming routine is more than just making your Cavalier King Charles Spaniel look like royalty. Grooming not only keeps your dog looking good, but it also keeps him feeling good. An effective grooming routine includes your dog's coat, nails, ears and teeth.

Grooming your Cavalier is an excellent way to spend quality time with him, and it also keeps you in touch with his overall health condition. It's extremely important to introduce your Cavalier to a grooming routine when he is a puppy. The sooner you make these grooming activities a part of your Cavalier's everyday life, the more cooperative he'll be.

BRUSHING A CAV'S COAT

Keeping your Cavalier's coat tangle-free does require some attention. Brush your dog's luxurious coat two to three times a week. You can get by with less, but it's easier to prevent tangles and knots from forming than to unravel them after the fact. There

Plaque builds up on your dog's teeth and forms tartar just like it does on yours.
Bacteria thrive in the pockets formed by the tartar under the gums and spread throughout the body. Some studies suggest that taking the time to brush your pet's teeth could actually extend her life.

it's a Fact

are many different types of dog brushes available, and whichever one you choose comes down to a matter of personal preference. However, for general brushing either a pin, bristle or slicker brush is recommended for the Cavalier's coat.

Start brushing at your dog's head and work your way toward the tail. Always brush in the direction that the hair lays. The Cav's biggest trouble spots for knots and tangles are the ears, the front of the chest and the leg fringe — especially where the top of the leg meets the chest and the tail feathering. It's important to pay close attention to each

of these areas and to carefully untangle any knots that you encounter. You should never bathe your dog with knots in his coat because the water will set these tangles, making them even more difficult to remove.

BATHING

In general, it's a good idea to bathe your Cavalier once or twice a month. Show dogs are usually bathed before every show, which could be as frequent as weekly, although it depends on the owner's preference.

If you give your dog his first bath when he's young, he'll become accustomed to the process. Wrestling a dog into the tub or chasing a freshly shampooed dog who has escaped from the bath will be no fun! Most dogs don't naturally enjoy their baths, but you at least want yours to cooperate with you throughout the ordeal.

Before bathing your dog, have the items that you'll need close at hand. First, decide where you will bathe him. You should use a tub or basin with a nonslip surface. Small dogs can even be bathed in a sink. In warm weather, some people like to use portable pools in their yards, although you'll want to make sure your dog doesn't head for the nearest dirt pile after his bath! You will also need a hose or shower spray to thoroughly wet his coat, shampoo and conditioner formulated for dogs, towels and perhaps a hair dryer. Human shampoos are too harsh for dogs' coats and will dry them out.

Before wetting the dog, brush him thoroughly to remove any dead hair, dirt and mats. Make sure he's at ease in the tub and set the water at a comfortable temperature. Begin by wetting his coat to the skin. Massage the shampoo into his coat, keeping it away from his face and eyes. Rinse him thoroughly, again avoiding his eyes and ears

Your Cavalier's beautiful coat needs at least twice-weekly brushing to stay sleek and tangle-free.

so no water gets into his ear canals. A thorough rinsing is important because shampoo residue dries out a dog's coat and makes him itchy. After you've rinsed out the shampoo, apply a conditioner made for your Cavalier's coat type. Always follow the product's directions, but conditioners typically need to be left on the coat for a minute or two. You can use this time to give your Cavalier a mini-massage. Thoroughly rinse the conditioner from your dog's coat and wrap him in a towel to absorb the initial moisture.

You can finish drying either with a second dry towel or a blow dryer set on low heat, held at a safe distance from your dog. Keep your dog indoors and away from drafts until he's completely dry. After the bathing process is complete, don't be surprised if your Cavalier runs around the house rubbing himself on carpet, rugs and sofas to get completely dry. You may want to confine your dog to one area of the house when it's bath time.

NAIL CLIPPING

Nail clipping is not a favorite pastime for many pups. With this in mind, acclimate your puppy to the procedure at a young age so he will sit patiently for his pedicures later in life. It can be very helpful to have an assistant hold your dog while you trim his nails. Not only can long nails scratch, but they'll cause your dog's feet to spread.

Some dogs' nails are worn down naturally by regular walking on hard surfaces, so the frequency with which you clip depends on your dog. Check his nails once a week; a good way to know when it's time for a trim is if you hear your dog's paws clicking as he walks across the floor.

There are several types of nail clippers and even electric grinding tools made for dogs. To start, have your clipper ready and some doggie treats on hand. You want your pup to view his clipping sessions in a positive light, and what better way to convince him than with food? Your assistant can comfort the pup and offer treats as you concentrate on the clipping itself. You'll also want to have styptic powder or some kind of blood-clotting agent on hand just in case.

First, it's important to understand that a blood vessel called the "quick" runs through each nail. You never want to cut into the quick, as it will bleed and is painful for your dog. When you look at your dog's nails, the quick is the pink area of the nail, and the white area is what you want to trim.

Start by grasping your pup's paw, add a little pressure to make the nail extend, so it is easier to clip. Clip off a little at a time to avoid cutting the quick, which is the dark area in the center of the nail. Praise your puppy and offer a treat with each nail. If you do cut the quick, which will cause bleeding,

Trim only the white area of your Cav's nails. The pink area, called the "quick," will bleed and hurt if you clip too closely. Keep styptic powder on hand in case of occasional accidents.

Every Cavalier deserves to look dapper. What do you need to keep your toy dog looking terrific? Go to Club Cav (**DogChannel. com/Club-Cav**) and download a checklist of essential grooming equipment you and your dog will need.

use styptic powder to lessen the blood flow. Don't panic or fuss, or you may frighten your Cavalier. Simply reassure your pup, stop the bleeding and move on to the next nail. You can also use this time to examine his footpads, making sure that they aren't dry or cracked and that nothing is embedded in them.

Many owners prefer the nail grinder. If you decide to use one, however, trim all the hair from around your Cavalier's feet and paw pads beforehand. Cavs definitely have "slippers" on their feet, and this hair can get caught in the head of the grinder and cause quite a mess for both you and your dog.

Some puppies may prefer the experience of the grinder to the clipper. It is less traumatic, and there's no chance of cutting through the quick. Use the grinder on a low setting and always talk soothingly to your dog throughout the procedure.

EAR CLEANING

While keeping your dog's ears clean unfortunately will not cause him to *hear* your cues any better, it will protect him from ear infection and ear-mite infestation. A dog's ears are vulnerable to waxy and foreign matter buildup. Check in your dog's ears reg-

ularly to ensure they look pink, clean and otherwise healthy. Even if they look fine, odor in the ears signals a problem and means it's time to call the vet.

A dog's ears should be cleaned regularly, about once a week. You can do this along with your regular brushing. Use a cotton ball or pad, and never probe into the ear canal while you wipe the ear gently. You can use an ear-cleansing liquid or powder available from your vet or pet-supply store, but you might prefer to use homemade solutions with ingredients like one part white vinegar and one part hydrogen peroxide. Ask your vet about home remedies before you attempt to concoct something on your own.

Keep your dog's ears free of excess hairs by plucking them as needed. If done gently, this will be painless for your dog. Look for wax, brown droppings (a sign of ear mites), redness or any other abnormalities. At the first sign of a problem, contact your vet so he can prescribe an appropriate medication.

EYE CARE

During grooming sessions, pay extra attention to the condition of your dog's eyes. If the area around the eyes is soiled or if tear staining has occurred, there are various cleaning agents made especially for this purpose. Look at your dog's eyes to make sure no debris has entered; dogs with large eyes and those who spend time outdoors are especially prone to this.

The signs of an eye infection are obvious: mucus, redness, puffiness, scabs or other signs of irritation. If your dog's eyes become infected, the veterinarian will likely prescribe an antibiotic ointment for treatment. If you notice signs of more serious problems, such as opacities in the eye, which usually

Brusha, brusha, brusha. Consistent oral care contributes to a dog's overall health.

Select a slicker brush that has pliable teeth. A slicker brush has rows of bent metal teeth that snag tangles so they can be worked out. You don't want to use one that is too stiff because it can injure your pet's skin. You also need a horsehair bristle brush, which will help to distribute the natural oils throughout your dog's coat. A metal comb helps keep the coat detangled, as well.

indicate cataracts, consult your vet at once. Taking time to pay attention to your Cavalier's eyes will alert you in the early stages of any problem so that you can get your dog treatment as soon as possible. It could save your dog's sight!

A CLEAN SMILE

Another essential part of grooming is brushing your dog's teeth and checking his overall oral condition. Studies show that about 80 percent of dogs experience dental problems by 2 years of age, and the percentage is higher in older dogs. Therefore, it is highly likely that your dog will have trouble with his teeth and gums unless you are proactive with his home dental care.

The most common canine dental problem is plaque buildup. If not treated, this can cause gum disease, infection or tooth loss. Bacteria from these infections can spread throughout the body, affecting the vital organs. Do you need any more convincing to start brushing your dog's teeth? If so, take a good whiff of your dog's breath and read on.

Fortunately, home dental care is rather easy and convenient for pet owners. Specially formulated canine toothpaste is easy to find. Be sure to use one of these toothpastes, not a product for humans. Some doggie pastes are even available in flavors appealing to dogs. If your dog likes the flavor, he will tolerate the process better, making things much easier for you! Toothpastes formulated for humans are not meant to be swallowed and can cause stomach upset in your dog.

Doggie toothbrushes come in different sizes and are designed to fit the contour of a canine mouth. Rubber fingertip brushes fit on your finger and have rubber nodes to clean the teeth and massage the gums. This may be easier to handle, as it is akin to rubbing your dog's teeth with your finger. If you have trouble finding a toothbrush small enough for your Cavalier's mouth, consider buying a human pediatric toothbrush; it should fit perfectly.

As with other grooming tasks, accustom your Cavalier pup to his dental care early on. Start gently, for a few minutes at a time, so that he gets used to the feel of the brush and you handling his mouth. Offer praise and petting so that he considers tooth-care time as a time when he gets extra love and attention. The routine should become second nature; he may not like it, but he should at least tolerate it.

Aside from brushing, offer dental toys to your dog and feed him crunchy biscuits, which help to minimize plaque. Rope toys have the added benefit of acting like floss as the dog chews. At your adult dog's yearly checkups, the veterinarian will likely perform a thorough tooth scraping, as well as a complete check for any problems. Proper care of your Cav's teeth will ensure that you'll enjoy your dog's smile for many years to come. The next time your dog gives you a kiss hello, you'll be glad you spent the time to care for his teeth.

NOTABLE & QUOTABLE

If you don't brush this breed for weeks on end, you are going to wish for a miracle. They shed and tangle, but with a little care, the coat is easily maintained. I brush my dogs on my lap in the evening. It doesn't take a lot of time if you keep up with it.

— Cavalier owner Pam Burkley of Ruther Glen, Va.

Chew toys can help keep your Cavalier's canines clean.

TAILS AND DEWCLAWS

Tail docking is optional on Cavalier King Charles Spaniels, but if done, it should be carried out within the first few days of life while still in the breeder's care, and one-third of the tail should remain. Docking of tails is now a subject under some debate, especially by veterinarians.

Dewclaws are usually removed when the puppy is only three or four days old. Cavaliers rarely have dewclaws on their hind legs, but they should always be checked so that they aren't left on unintentionally. Removal of dewclaws is an aesthetic consideration, but it also avoids the possibility that these nonfunctional claws might get torn. However, many breeders no longer remove the front dewclaws because leaving them intact rarely leads to any problems. When purchasing a puppy, make a note to ask whether the puppy's dewclaws have been removed. If they haven't, then you'll also need to clip your Cavalier's nails on the front dewclaws when it is time to clip his other nails.

> **Did You Know?**
>
> **Weekly brushing with your slicker helps keep a shedding coat off your clothes and furniture.** Follow the slicker with the bristle brush to distribute the natural oils throughout your Cav's coat. Pull a comb through his hair to confirm that all the tangles are removed.

10 Steps to Flea Control

1 Make sure your Cavalier is scratching because she has fleas instead of another reason. Search her belly area for small black insects. Brush her on a dark cloth to reveal fleas; the eggs drop off and show up as white sandy-looking particles.

2 Schedule to treat your house, yard and Cavalier the same day. Make coinciding appointments with the exterminator and your groomer so your pet will be at the groomer while the house is treated. Wash all bedding, including your Cavalier's.

3 Speak to your veterinarian about the safest method of flea treatment for your Cavalier. If you choose a spot-on treatment, don't allow your groomer to also use a chemical dip on your pet. Both are insecticides, and you don't want to overdose your dog with too many chemicals.

4 One flea can lay up to 30 eggs a day. If you choose to use the aerosol bombs (available from pet-supply stores) to treat your home, select the brands with an insect growth regulator. This chemical prevents the flea eggs from hatching.

5 Spray your yard with insecticide either early in the morning or late in the afternoon. Avoid applying it in the heat of the sun because it dries out too quickly to be effective.

6 Once your Cavalier is flea-free, don't take her into flea-infested areas during flea season (spring and summer). This could include parks (yes, dog parks) and the yards and homes of friends, neighbors or relatives.

7 Use a flea comb (which has very closely set teeth) and have a cup of water with a teaspoon of cooking oil mixed in standing nearby. Draw the comb through your dog's coat; if it captures a flea, drop the insect into the water. The oil will smother it.

8 Check your dog's stool for evidence of tapeworms (small, flat segments that look like grains of rice) after an infestation. Fleas are part of the tapeworm cycle.

9 Fleas will bite you and your family, as well as your pets. Keeping your Cavalier flea-free will prevent your children and other household members from getting bitten by the insects.

10 Cut up a flea collar and put the pieces in your vacuum bag, then run the vacuum frequently. The cut-up pieces will kill any fleas sucked into the bag.

A TOY

Reward-based training methods instruct dogs on what to do and help them do it correctly, setting them up for success and rewards rather than mistakes and punishment.

Most dogs find food rewards meaningful; Cavalier King Charles Spaniels are no exception, as they tend to be motivated by food. This works well because positive training relies on using treats, at least initially, to encourage your dog to demonstrate a certain behavior. The treat is then given as a reward. When you reinforce desired behaviors with rewards that are valuable to your dog, you are met with happy cooperation rather than resistance.

Positive reinforcement does not necessarily equal passivity. While you are rewarding your Cavalier's desirable behaviors, you must still manage him to be sure he isn't getting rewarded for his undesirable behaviors.

Training tools, such as leashes, tethers, baby gates and crates, help keep your dog out of trouble. The use of force-free negative punishment (the dog's behavior makes a good thing go away) helps him realize there are negative consequences for inappropriate behaviors.

Did You Know?

Your Cav's stomach is small. Use small pieces of treats and cut back on regular meal amounts to avoid stuffing his face before training is over and to avoid unwanted weight gain.

CLICKER TRAINING

Clicker training is a precise way to mark a desired behavior so an animal knows exactly what behavior earned a reward. A clicker is a small, plastic device that makes a sharp clicking sound when a button is pressed. You can purchase one at any pet-supply store. You "charge" the clicker by clicking and giving your Cavalier a treat several times, until he understands that the click means a treat is forthcoming. The click then becomes a secondary reinforcer. It's not the reward itself, but it will become so closely linked in your dog's mind with a reward that it has the same effect.

Next, click the clicker when your Cavalier does any desirable behavior. Then, follow it up with a click and treat. The click exactly marks (more precisely than a word or gesture) the desired behavior, quickly teaching your dog which behaviors will earn rewards.

DOGGIE MANNERS

Every Cav should be trained in the basics: sit, down, stay, come and heel. A dog with a solid understanding of these basic cues will be a more pleasant companion to live with.

When teaching your Cavalier King Charles Spaniel these exercises, you have two choices: You can work with your dog on your own, or you can attend obedience classes. The advantages of an obedience class are that your Cavalier will have to learn amid the distractions of other people and dogs and that the trainer can quickly correct your mistakes. Having the presence of a qualified instructor and other handlers who may have more canine experience than you is another advantage of the obedience class environment. The instructor and other handlers can help you to find the most efficient way of teaching your dog a cue or exercise. It's often easier to learn by other people's mistakes than by making your own.

CHOOSING A TRAINER

Anyone can say that he or she is a dog trainer. There is no standard licensing or certification that is required by law. Therefore, you must be very careful about choosing a trainer for your puppy. An inexperienced or misinformed dog trainer can wreak havoc on the behavior of your Cavalier. When choosing a dog trainer, take your time, be choosy and trust your instincts. Ultimately you are in charge of your dog's training, so don't let any trainer talk you into doing something that you are not comfortable with.

Use these tips before choosing a trainer:

✔ Get recommendations from your veterinarian or friends.

✔ Once you find a trainer, observe a class and watch the interactions.

✔ Ask the trainer about his or her experience and training methods.

✔ Ask the trainer if he or she participates in continuing education classes.

✔ Find out if the trainer has been certified by any training organization or is a member of a training organization, such as the Association of Pet Dog Trainers.

✔ Ask if there are separate classes for puppies and adult dogs.

✔ Inquire if the trainer offers any handouts in class.

✔ Ask if proof of vaccination is required.

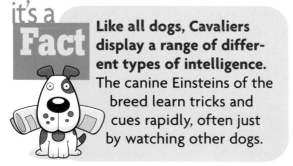

it's a Fact Like all dogs, Cavaliers display a range of different types of intelligence. The canine Einsteins of the breed learn tricks and cues rapidly, often just by watching other dogs.

Use small morsels of treats when training your dog. It should be just a taste of the rewards that come with good behavior.

PUPPY KINDERGARTEN

Most owners will want to enroll their dogs in a puppy kindergarten course followed by a basic obedience classes. In puppy kindergarten, your Cav will be in a class with various breeds of puppies in his age range (up to 5 months old). It's a great way for him to learn the correct way (as well as the wrong ways) to interact with other dogs and their people.

For a first-time puppy owner, these invaluable socialization classes are the building blocks for more training later. Your Cavalier puppy will be considerably smaller than, say, a Golden Retriever puppy at 4 or 5 months of age. While you do want your puppy to socialize with other dogs, it's also important for him to be safe. Most training facilities offer puppy classes by size, so make sure to ask for a puppy class for small or toy dogs.

THE SIT CUE

There are several ways to teach your puppy to sit. The first one is to catch him whenever he is about to sit; then, as his backside nears the floor, say "sit," praise and reward. If your timing's right, he'll make the connection between the verbal cue and the action.

Another method is to start with your puppy on his leash in front of you. Show him a treat in the palm of your right hand. Bring your hand up under his nose and, almost in slow motion, move your hand up and back so his nose goes up in the air and his head tilts back as he follows the treat in your hand. At that point, he will have to either sit or fall over; so

as his back legs buckle under, say "sit," praise and reward. You may have to begin with your hand lightly running up his chest, actually lifting his chin up until he sits. Some (usually older) dogs require gentle pressure on their hindquarters. Puppies generally don't appreciate this physical dominance.

After a few times, you should be able to show your dog a treat in the open palm of your hand; raise your hand to waist height as you give the cue. Once again, you have taught him two things at the same time. Both the verbal cue and the motion of the hand are signals for the sit. Your puppy is watching you almost more than he is listening to you, so what you do is just as important as what you say.

Don't save these drills for training sessions only. Use them as much as possible during everyday activities. Your Cavalier should always sit before receiving his food dish. He should also sit to let you go through a doorway first, when the doorbell rings or when you stop to speak to someone on the street.

Keep your actions consistent as you train your dog. She'll be watching your movements just as much as she'll be listening to what you say.

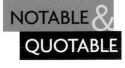

NOTABLE & QUOTABLE

If you like a dog trainer, chances are he or she will be good for you. You can learn better from someone you like who is kind and patient than from someone who is obviously good but difficult to communicate with. Remember, it doesn't matter how many titles their dog has if they can't teach you how to train your dog the basics. The ability to teach, communicate and empathize is essential for a good instructor.
— *Gerilyn J. Bielakiewicz, a certified professional dog trainer at Canine University in Malden, Mass.*

THE DOWN CUE

Before teaching the down cue, consider how the dog feels about this exercise. To him, "down" is a submissive position. Being flat on the floor with you standing over him isn't his idea of fun. It's up to you to let him know that, while it may not be fun, the reward of your approval is worth his effort.

Start with the puppy on your left side in a sit position. Hold the leash right above his collar in your left hand. Have an extra-special treat, such as a small piece of cooked chicken or a small slice of hot dog, in your right hand. Place it at the end of the pup's nose, then steadily move your hand down and forward along the ground. Hold the leash to prevent a sudden lunge for the food. As the puppy goes into the down position, say "down" very gently.

The difficulty with this exercise is twofold: it's the submissive aspect and the fact that most people say the cue as if they are drill sergeants in charge of recruits! So issue the cue sweetly, give your pup the treat and have him maintain the down position for several seconds. If he tries to get up immediately, place your hands on his shoulders, then press down gently and praise him quietly. As you progress with this lesson, increase the "down time" until he will hold it until you say "OK" (his cue for release). Practice this one in the house at various times throughout the day.

By increasing the length of time during which your dog must maintain the down position, you'll find many uses for it. For example, he can lie at your feet in the vet's office (or anywhere that both of you have to wait), when you are on the phone, while the family is eating and so forth. If you progress to training for competitive obedience, he'll already have mastered the exercise called the "long down."

SMART TIP!

Before you begin your puppy's education, accustom her to her collar and leash. Choose a collar for your pup that's secure but not heavy or bulky. She won't enjoy training if she's uncomfortable. A flat buckle collar is fine for everyday wear and for training. Never use a choke or prong collar. Most trainers prefer a lightweight 6-foot woven cotton or nylon training leash because it's easy to fold up in your hand and comfortable to hold because there is a certain amount of give to it.

THE STAY CUE

You can teach your Cavalier to stay in the sit, down and stand positions. To teach the sit/stay, have your dog sit on your left side. Hold the leash at waist height in your left hand and let your dog know that you have a treat in your right hand. Step forward on your right foot as you say "stay." Immediately turn and stand directly in front of your dog, keeping your right hand up high so he'll keep his eye on the treat hand and maintain the sit position for about five seconds. Return to your original position and offer the reward.

Increase the length of the sit/stay each time until your dog can hold it for at least 30 seconds without moving. After about a week of success, move out on your right foot and take two steps before turning to face the dog. Give the stay hand signal (left palm back toward the dog's head) as you leave. He gets the treat when you return and he holds the sit/stay. Increase the distance that you walk away from him before turning until you reach the length of your training leash.

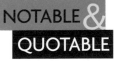
NOTABLE & QUOTABLE

People often are under the misunderstanding that only big dogs need training, but that's certainly not the case.

Whether you have a Labrador Retriever or a Papillion, if you drop a glass on the kitchen floor, you need to have a cue in place so that your dog doesn't walk through the glass shards and hurt his paws. And while it's fashionable to carry small dogs rather than let them walk on a leash, should he run out into the road, cars don't discriminate in hazardous situations.

— New Jersey-based behaviorist and trainer Kathy Santo

Don't rush it! Go back to the beginning if he moves before he should.

No matter what the lesson, never be upset by having to back up a few steps. The repetition and practice are what will make your dog reliable in these cues. It won't do any good to move on to something more difficult if your dog doesn't master the cue at the easier levels. Above all, even if you do get frustrated, never let your puppy know! Always keep a positive, upbeat attitude during training sessions.

The down/stay is taught in the same way once your dog is completely reliable with the down cue. Again, don't rush it. With your dog in the down position on your left side, step out on your right foot as you say "stay." Return by walking around in back of the dog and into your original position. While you are training, it's OK to murmur something to encourage him to stay put. Once your dog will stay without moving when you are 3 or 4 feet away, begin to increase the length of time before you return. Be sure he holds the down on your return until you say "OK." At that point, he gets his treat — just so he'll remember for next time that it's not over until you say it's over.

THE COME CUE

No cue is more important to the safety of your Cav than "come." It's what you should say every single time you see your pup running toward you: say your dog's name, the cue, praise and reward. During playtime, run a few feet away, then turn and say the cue as your pup is already running to you. You can go so far as to teach him two things at once if you squat down and hold out your arms. As the pup gets close to you and you're saying "good dog," bring your right arm in about waist high. Now he's also learning the hand signal, an excellent device should you

SMART TIP!

If you always train while standing up, you're guaranteed to end up with a backache. Especially when teaching stationary exercises, sitting on the floor with your dog will save your back and make you appear less intimidating. You can also work with your Cavalier while you sit in a chair, or put the dog on a comfortable raised surface such as a table, sofa or bed. When she understands the exercises, you can go back to standing up while you train.

be on the phone when you need to get him to come to you! You'll also both be one step ahead when you enter obedience classes.

When your puppy responds to your well-timed cue, try it with him on his training leash. This time, catch him off guard; while he's sniffing a leaf or watching a bird, say your dog's name and the cue. You may have to pause for a split second after you say his name to be sure you have his attention. If your puppy shows any sign of confusion, give the leash a mild tug and take a couple of steps backward. Do not repeat the cue. In this case, just praise him as he reaches you.

That's the No. 1 training rule: Each cue is given only once. Anything more and your puppy might not pay attention. You'll also notice that all cues are only one word. Even when they are actually two words, you should say them as one.

Never call your dog to come to you — with or without using his name — if you are angry or intend to correct him for some misbehavior. When correcting your pup, you should go to him. Your dog must connect any cue with something pleasant and with your approval; then you can rely on his response.

Teaching your Cavalier to heel will make your time together a walk in the park.

Puppies, like children, have notoriously short attention spans, so don't overdo it with any of your training sessions. Keep each lesson short. Break it up with a quick run around the yard or a ball toss, repeat the lesson and quit as soon as the pup gets it right. That way, you'll always end on a positive note.

Life isn't perfect and neither are puppies. A time will come, often around 10 months of age, when your puppy choose to "forget" his name. He may respond by wagging his tail (and even seeming to smile at you) with a look that says "Make me!" Laugh, throw his favorite toy and skip the lesson you had planned that day. Pups will be pups!

THE HEEL CUE

The second most important cue to teach is heel. When you are walking your growing puppy, you need to be in control. Besides, it looks terrible to be pulled and yanked down the street, and it's not much fun either. Your 8- to 10-week-old puppy will probably follow you everywhere, but that's his natural instinct, not your control over the situation. However, any time he does follow you, you can say "heel" and be ahead of the game, as he will learn to associate this cue with the action of following you before you even begin teaching him to heel.

There is a very precise, almost military, procedure for teaching your dog to heel. As with all other obedience training, begin with the dog on your left side. He will be in a very nice sit, and you will have the training leash across your chest. Hold the loop and folded leash in your right hand. Pick up the leash slack above the dog in your left hand and hold it loosely at your side. Step out on your left foot as you say "heel." If the puppy does not move, give a gentle tug or pat your left leg to get him started. If he surges ahead of you, stop and pull him back gently until he's at your side. Tell him to sit and begin again.

Walk a few steps and stop while the puppy is correctly beside you. Tell him to sit and give mild verbal praise. (More enthusiastic praise will encourage him to think the lesson is over.) Repeat the lesson, increasing the number of steps you take only as long as the dog is heeling nicely beside you. When you end the lesson, have him hold the sit, then give him the "OK" to let him know that this is the end of the lesson. Praise him so that he knows he did a good job.

The cure for excessive pulling (a common problem) is to stop when the dog is no more than 2 or 3 feet ahead of you. Guide him back into position and begin again. With a really determined puller, try switching to a head collar. This will automatically turn the pup's head toward you so you can bring him back easily to the heel position. Give quiet, reassuring praise every time the leash goes slack, and he stays with you.

Staying and heeling can take a lot out of a dog, so provide playtime and free-running exercise to shake off the stress when the lessons are over. You don't want him to associate training with all work and no fun.

TAPERING OFF TIDBITS

Your dog has been watching you — and the hand that treats — throughout all of his lessons, but now it's time to break the treat habit. Begin by giving your Cav treats only at the end of each lesson. Then start to give a treat after the end of only some of the lessons. At the end of every lesson, as well as during them, be consistent with your praise. Your puppy won't know whether he'll get a treat or not, but he should keep performing well just in case! Finally, you will stop giving him treat rewards entirely. Save the food for something brand new that you want to teach him. Keep up the praise, and you'll always have a "good dog."

CHAPTER 10

CAVS GONE

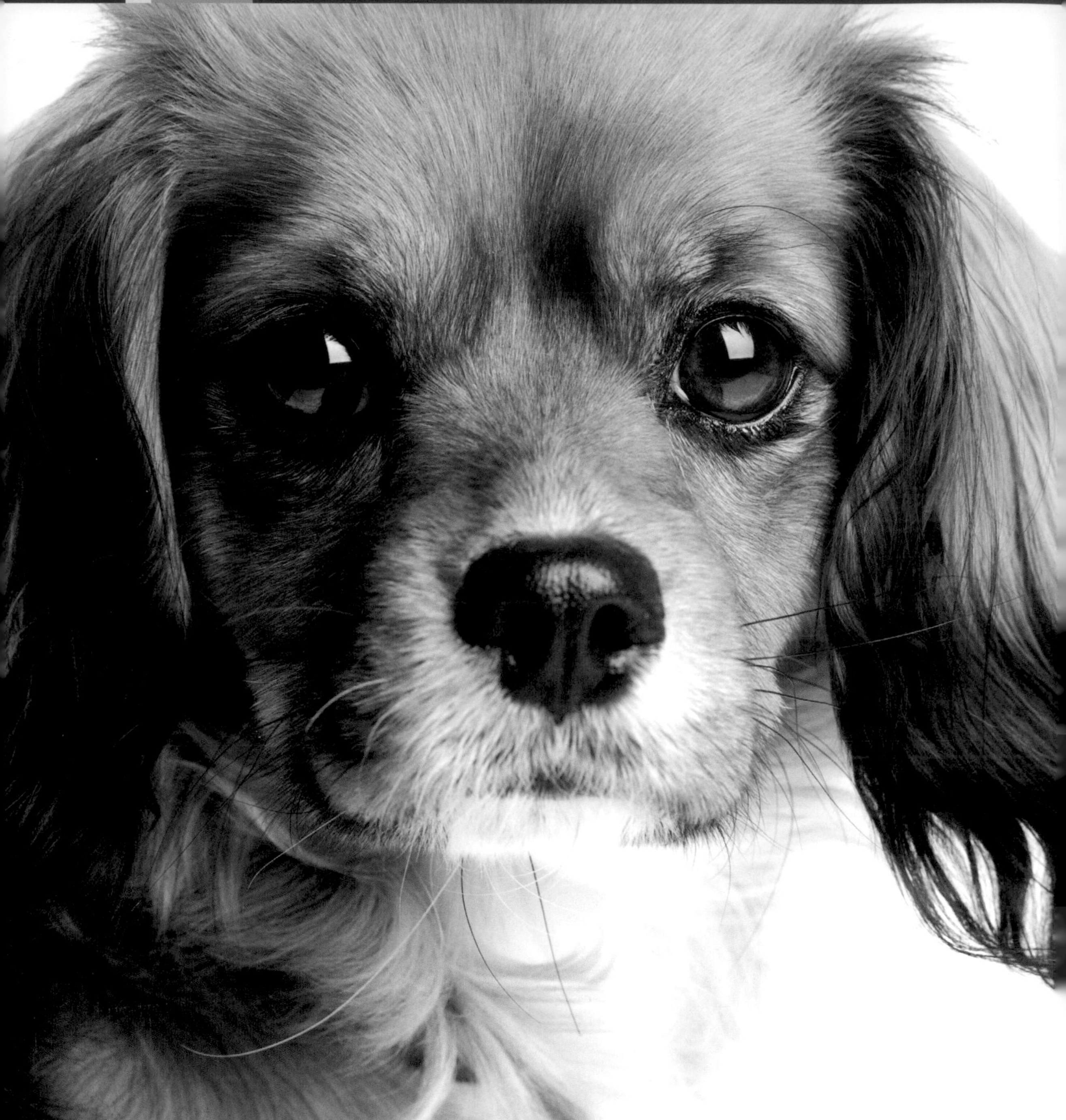

WILD

Discipline — training one to act in accordance with rules — brings order to life. It's as simple as that. Without discipline, particularly in a group society, chaos reigns supreme and the group will eventually perish. Humans and canines are social animals and need some form of discipline in order to function effectively. Dogs need discipline in their lives in order to understand how their pack (you and other family members) functions and how they must act in order to survive.

Living with an untrained spaniel is a lot like owning a piano that you do not know how to play. It's a nice object to look at, but it doesn't do much more than that to bring your life pleasure. Now, try taking piano lessons, and suddenly the piano comes alive bringing forth magical sounds and rhythms that set your heart singing and your body swaying.

The same is true of your Cav. Every dog is a big responsibility and, if not trained, may develop unacceptable behaviors that annoy you or cause family friction.

To train your Cavalier, you can enroll in an obedience class to teach him good manners as you learn how and why he behaves the way he does. You will also find out how to communicate with your Cav and how to recognize and understand his communications with you. Suddenly your dog takes on a new role in your life; he is interesting, smart, well behaved and fun to be with. He demonstrates his bond of devotion to you daily. In other words, your Cavalier does wonders for your ego because he constantly reminds you that you are not only his leader, you are his hero!

Those involved with teaching dog obedience and counseling owners about their dogs' behavior have discovered interesting facts about dog ownership. For example, training dogs when they are puppies results in the highest success rate in developing well-mannered and well-adjusted adult. Training an older Cavalier King Charles Spaniel, from 6 months to 6 years, can produce almost equal results, providing that the owner accepts the dog's slower learning rate and is willing to patiently work to help him succeed. Unfortunately, many owners of untrained adult dogs lack the patience necessary, so they don't persist until their dogs are successful at learning particular behaviors.

Training a 10- to 16-week-old Cavalier puppy (20 weeks maximum) is like working with a dry sponge in a pool of water.

Did You Know?

Some dogs bark because they are distressed, bored or lonely. Isolated dogs are especially prone to barking nonstop. The best remedy is to bring them inside so they can share daily activities with the rest of the family. Give your dog something to do that's more fun than barking. It's difficult to bark when you're busy chewing a bone or working the food out of a treat toy. Also, make sure she has plenty of exercise. She can't bark while she sleeps!

The pup soaks up whatever you teach him and constantly looks for more to do and learn. At this early age, his body is not yet producing hormones, and therein lies the reason for such a high success rate. Without hormones, he is focused on you and is not particularly interested in investigating other places, dogs, people, etc.

You are his leader; his provider of food, water, shelter and security. Your Cavalier latches onto you and wants to stay close. He usually will follow you from room to room, won't let you out of his sight when you are outdoors with him and will respond in like manner to the people and animals you encounter. If you greet a friend warmly, he will happily greet the person as well. If, however, you are hesitant, even anxious, about the approaching stranger, he will also respond accordingly.

Once your Cavalier puppy begins to produce hormones, his natural curiosity emerges and he begins to investigate the world around him. It is at this time when you may notice your untrained dog begins to wander away and ignore your cues to stay close.

Whether your new spaniel is a pup or a mature adult, the teaching methods and training techniques used in basic behaviors are the same. No dog, whether puppy or adult, likes harsh or inhumane training methods. All creatures, however, respond favorably to gentle motivational methods and sincere praise and encouragement.

The following behavioral issues are those most commonly encountered. Remember, every dog and situation is unique. Because behavioral abnormalities are the leading reason for owners' abandoning their pets, we hope that you will make a valiant effort to solve your Cavalier King Charles Spaniel's behavioral issues.

SMART TIP!

Cats are the pets most likely to arouse your puppy's interest. Besides all the other reasons you shouldn't let your puppy have run of the house, your cat is yet another. This is your cat's house, and cats are territorial. Having a new puppy invade your cat's territory isn't going to make things easier. When you do start letting your puppy see more of the house, keep her on a leash and don't let her get into the cat's special places.

SEPARATION ANXIETY

Any behaviorist will tell you that separation anxiety is the most common problem pet owners complain about. It is also one of the easiest to prevent. Unfortunately, owners don't usually consult behaviorists until their dogs are stressed-out, neurotic messes. At that stage, it is indeed a problem that requires the help of a professional.

To avoid this anxiety, train your puppy to accept people in the house coming and going. Leaving your puppy in his crate or a confined area while family members come and go — and stay away for longer and longer periods of time — is the basic way to desensitize him to the family's frequent departures. If you are at home most of every day, make it a point to go out for at least an hour or two whenever possible.

How you leave is vital to your dog's reaction. He's no fool. He knows the difference between your sweats and business suits, jeans and dresses. He sees you pat your pocket to check for your wallet, check that you have your cell phone or pick up the car keys. He knows from the hurry of the kids in

The best way to get your Cavalier well socialized is to introduce her to different kinds of people and situations. Have her meet a man with a beard, take her to a dog-friendly restaurant, take her for a ride in the car. Go online to download a socialization checklist at **DogChannel.com/Club-Cav**

the morning that they're off to school until afternoon. Lipstick? Aftershave lotion? Lunch boxes? Every move you make registers in his sensory perception and memory. Your puppy knows more about your departures than the FBI. You can't get away with anything!

Before you leave the house, check your dog's water bowl and his toy supply. You may want to turn the radio or TV on low. Confine your dog to his own area; his crate or exercise pen. Your dog should be safe when he is alone in the house, and if he has too much room to roam, he'll find some mischief. Don't give him access to a window where he can watch you leave the house.

When you are ready to leave, don't give your Cavalier a big hug and a fond farewell. Don't drag out a long goodbye. This will only jump-start his separation anxiety. Toss a biscuit into your dog's area, say goodbye and close the door. He may bark a couple of times or maybe whine a bit, but he should settle down to enjoy his biscuit and take a nap. Eventually, the barks and whines will stop because he knows the routine.

This is similar to when you first trained your puppy to happily spend time in his crate. You left him in his crate for increasing increments to acclimate him to his special place. If he has separation anxiety issues at any time in the future, refresh his memory by going back to that basic training.

Now comes your return. Don't make a big production of coming home. Just say "hi." Once you've taken off your hat and coat and glanced at the mail — and your dog has settled down from the excitement of seeing you return — go and give him a friendly greeting. He may need to go potty, and some play time or a walk are good rewards for his time well spent alone.

DIGGING

Digging is another natural and normal doggie behavior. Wild dogs dig to bury whatever food they can save to eat later. (And you thought *we* invented the "doggie bag"!) Burying bones or toys is a primary cause to dig. Dogs also dig to get at interesting little underground creatures like moles and mice. In the summer, they dig to get down to cooler earth. In the winter, they dig to get beneath the cold surface to warmer earth.

The solution to the last two is easy: In the summer, provide a bed that's up off the ground and placed in a shaded area. In the winter, your dog should either sleep indoors or be given an adequate insulated doghouse outdoors. To understand how natural and normal this is, you only have to consider the Nordic breeds of sled dog who, at the end of the run, routinely dig a bed for themselves in the snow. It's the nesting instinct. How often have you seen your dog go round and round in circles, pawing at his blanket or bedding before flopping down to sleep?

Domesticated dogs also dig to escape, and that's a lot more dangerous than it is destructive. A dog that digs under the fence is the one that is hit by a car or becomes lost. A good fence to protect a digger should be

it's a Fact

Sharing your Cavalier King Charles Spaniel's accomplishments with others pleases them as much as it does you. An adorable little toy dog cheerfully doing tricks boosts everyone's morale. Nursing homes, hospitals, pet demos, animal charity fundraisers and countless other facilities welcome such an upbeat little attention-getter.

set 10 to 12 inches below ground level, and every fence needs to be routinely checked for even the smallest openings that can become possible escape routes.

Catching your dog in the act of digging is the easiest way to stop it because your dog will make the "one-plus-one" connection. Digging, however, is too often a solitary occupation, something the lonely dog does out of boredom. Catch your young puppy in the act and put a stop to it before you have a yard full of craters. It's more difficult to stop if your dog sees you gardening. If you can dig, why can't he? Because you say so, that's why! Some dogs are excavation experts, and some dogs never dig. However, when it comes to any of these instinctive canine behaviors, never say "never."

BARKING

Here's a big, noisy problem! Telling a dog he must never bark is like telling a child never to speak! Consider how confusing it must be to your dog that you are using your voice (which is your form of barking) to teach him when to bark and when not to! That is precisely the reason not to "bark back" when the dog's barking is annoying you (or your neighbors). Try to understand the scenario from the dog's viewpoint. He barks. You bark. He barks again; you bark again. This conversation can go on forever!

The first time your adorable little puppy said "yip" or "yap," you were ecstatic. His first word! You smiled, told him how smart he was and allowed him to do it. So there's that one-plus-one thing again because he will understand by your happy reaction that "my alpha loves it when I talk." Ignore his barking in the beginning and allow it, but don't encourage barking during play. Instead, use the "put a toy in it" method to tone it down. Very softly, say "quiet" as you hand off the toy. If the barking continues, stand up straight, fold your arms and turn your back on the dog. If he barks, you won't play, and you should follow the same rule for all undesirable behavior during play.

Dogs bark in reaction to sounds and sights. Another dog's bark, a person passing by or even just rustling leaves can set off a barker. If someone coming up your driveway or to your door provokes a barking frenzy, use the saturation method to stop it. Have several friends come and go every three or four minutes over as long a period of time as they can spare (it could take a couple of hours). Attach about a foot of rope to the dog's collar and have very small treats handy. Each time a car pulls up or a person approaches, let the dog bark once (grab the rope if you need to physically restrain him), say "OK, good dog," give him a treat and make him sit. "OK" is the release cue. It lets the dog know that he has alerted you and tells him that you are now in charge. That person leaves and the next arrives, and so on until everyone — especially the dog — is bored and the barking has stopped.

Don't forget to thank your friends. Your neighbors, by the way, may be more than willing to assist you in this parlor game.

Excessive barking outdoors is more difficult to keep in check because, when it happens, the dog is probably outside while you are inside. A few warning barks are fine, but use the same method to tell him when enough is enough. You will have to stay outside with him for that bit of training.

There is one more kind of vocalization that is called "idiot barking" (from idiopathic, meaning "of unknown cause"). It is usually rhythmic or a timed series of barks.

You can put a stop to it immediately by calling your Cavalier to come. This form of barking can drive neighbors crazy and commonly occurs when a dog is left outside at night or for long periods of time during the day. He is completely and thoroughly bored! A change of scenery may help, such as relocating him to a room indoors when he is used to being outside. A few new toys or different dog biscuits might be the solution. If he is left alone and no one can get home during the day, a noontime walk with a local dog sitter would be the perfect solution.

FOOD-RELATED PROBLEMS

We're not talking about eating, diets or nutrition here, we're talking about bad habits. Face it: All dogs are beggars. Food is the motivation for everything we want our dogs to do and, when you combine that with their innate ability to "con" us in order to get their way, it's a wonder there aren't far more obese dogs in the world.

Who can resist the bleeding-heart look that says "I'm starving," or the paw that gently pats your knee when he gives you a knowing look, or the whining "Please?" or even the total body language of a perfect sit beneath the cookie jar. Anyone who professes to love his dog would have a difficult time consistently turning down the pleas of his clever canine's performances. One thing is for sure, though: Definitely do not allow begging at the table. Family meals should not include your dog.

Control your dog's begging habit by making him work for his rewards. Ignore his begging when you can. Utilize the obedience cues you've taught him. Use "off" for the pawing. Performing a sit or even a long down will interrupt the whining. His reward in these situations definitely shouldn't be a treat! Casual verbal praise is enough. Be sure all members of the family follow the same rules.

There is a different type of begging that does demand your immediate response, and that is the appeal to be let (or taken) outside! Usually, that is a quick paw or small whine to get your attention, followed by a race to the door. This type of begging needs your quick attention and approval. Of course, a really smart dog will soon figure out how to cut you off at the pass and direct you to that cookie jar on your way to the door! Some dogs are always one step ahead of us.

Stealing food is a problem only if you aren't paying attention. A dog can't steal food that's not within his reach. Leaving your dog in the kitchen with the roast beef on the table is asking for trouble. There's nothing idiopathic about this problem, although it is perhaps a little idiotic! Putting cheese and crackers on the coffee table also requires a watchful eye to stop the thief in his tracks. The word to use (one word, remember, even if it's two words pronounced as one) is "Leave it!" Instead of preceding it with yet another "No!" try using a guttural sound like "Aagh!" It sounds more like a warning growl to the dog and therefore has instant meaning.

Canine thieves are in their element when little kids are carrying cookies in their hands! Your dog will think he's been exceptionally clever if he causes a child to drop a cookie. Bonanza! The easiest solution is to keep the dog and children separated from each other at snack time. You must also be sure that the kids understand that they shouldn't tease the dog with food — his or theirs. Your dog won't mean to bite the kids, but when he snatches at a tidbit so near the level of his mouth, it can result in an unintended nip.

EATING EXCREMENT

The unpleasant subject of dogs eating their own feces (known as coprophagia) can be dealt with relatively easily, even though no one is exactly sure why dogs do this. Some say it's primordial, while others think that it indicates a lack of something in the diet (but there's no agreement as to what that "something" is). Unless the dog has worms, eating feces can't make him sick, but that's no reason to allow it to continue. There are products said to alleviate the problem, but check with your vet before you add anything to your dog's diet. Sprinkling hot pepper on the feces is an after-the-fact solution. Prevention is the better way to go.

When you housetrained your dog, you took him outside on a leash and stayed with him until he did his business. Afterward, you moved him away or took him back indoors, while you went back and cleaned up the feces. You were not giving him any opportunity to indulge in this strange canine habit. Now that your dog goes outside alone, watch to make sure he doesn't start. At his first sign of interest in his own excrement, or that of

NOTABLE & QUOTABLE

Most toy breeds are exceptionally intelligent dogs who catch on to training very quickly. Studies show that people who continue to use their brains into their older age live longer, healthier lives, and I believe this holds true for dogs, as well.

— Deborah Wood, a trainer from Beaverton, Ore.

any other animal, give him a sharp "No! Leave it!" and then bring the dog indoors so you can clean up. To clean up after your dog on the street, use a plastic bag over your hand to pick up the feces. In your yard, a poop-scooper is the easiest answer.

Cat feces entices many dogs, possibly because it has a different, often fishy, odor. If you have cats, consider using the litter boxes that are made with narrow tunnel entrances to deter all but the most insistent of dogs. Keep the litter clean and the box in a spot that's inaccessible to your dog.

CHEWING AND NIPPING

Nipping at fingers and toes is normal puppy behavior. Chewing is also the way that puppies investigate their surroundings. However, you'll have to teach your puppy that chewing anything other than his toys isn't acceptable. That won't happen overnight, and at times puppy teeth will test your patience because they are as sharp as little needles. However, if you allow nipping and

chewing to continue, just think about the damage that a mature Cavalier can do with a full set of adult teeth.

Whenever your puppy nips your hand or fingers, cry out "Ouch!" in a loud voice, which should startle your puppy and stop him from nipping, even if only for a moment. Immediately distract him by offering a small treat or an appropriate toy for him to chew instead (which means having chew toys and puppy treats handy or in your pockets at all times). Praise him when he takes the toy and tell him what a good dog he is. Praise is just as (or even more) important in puppy training as discipline and correction.

Puppies also tend to nip at children more often than at adults, since they perceive little ones to be more vulnerable and more similar to their littermates. Teach your children appropriate responses to the dog's nipping behavior. If they are unable to handle it themselves, you may have to intervene. Puppy nips can be quite painful and a child's frightened reaction will only encourage a puppy to nip harder, which is a natural canine response. As with all other puppy situations, always supervise all interactions between your Cavalier puppy and children.

Chewing on objects, not just family members' fingers and ankles, is also normal canine behavior that can be especially tedious (for the owner, not the pup) during the teething period when the puppy's adult teeth are growing in. At this stage, chewing just plain feels good. Furniture legs and cabinet corners are common puppy favorites. Shoes and other personal items also taste pretty good to a pup.

Once again, the best solution is prevention. If you value something, keep it tucked away and out of reach. You can't hide your dining-room table in a closet, but you can try to deflect the chewing by applying a bitter product made just to deter dogs from chewing. Available in a spray or cream, this substance is vile-tasting (although safe for dogs), and most puppies will avoid the forbidden object after one tiny taste. You can also apply the product to your leather leash if the puppy tries to chew on his lead during leash-training sessions.

Keep a ready supply of safe chews handy to offer your Cavalier as a distraction when he starts to chew on something that's off-limits. Remember that at this tender age, he doesn't yet know what is permitted or forbidden, so you have to be "on call" every minute he's awake and on the prowl.

You may lose a treasure or two during your puppy's growth period, and the furniture might sustain a nasty nick or two. These can be trying times, so be prepared for those inevitable accidents and comfort yourself in knowing that this too shall pass.

JUMPING UP

Cavalier puppies aren't known to be notorious jumpers,. They are, however, still puppies after all, and puppies jump up … on you, your guests, your counters and your furniture.

Just another normal part of growing up, and one you need to meet head-on before it becomes an ingrained habit.

The key to jump correction is consistency. You can't correct your Cavalier for jumping up on you today then allow it to happen tomorrow by greeting him with hugs and kisses. As you have learned by now, consistency is critical to all puppy lessons.

For starters, try turning your back as soon as your puppy jumps. Jumping up is a means of gaining your attention and, if the pup can't see your face, he may get discouraged and learn that he loses eye contact with his beloved master when he jumps up.

Leash corrections also work, and most puppies respond well to a leash tug if they jump. Grasp the leash close to the puppy's collar and give a quick tug downward, using the cue "off." Don't use the word "down," since down is used to teach the puppy to lie down, which is a separate action that he will learn during his education in the basic cues. As soon as your puppy has backed off, tell him to sit and immediately praise him for doing so. This will take many repetitions and won't be accomplished quickly, so don't get discouraged or give up; you must be even more persistent than your puppy.

A second method used for jump correction is the spritzer bottle. Fill a spray bottle with water mixed with a bit of lemon juice or vinegar. As soon as puppy jumps, command him "off" and spritz him with the water mixture. Of course, that means having the spray bottle handy whenever or wherever jumping usually happens.

Yet a third method to discourage jumping is grasping the puppy's paws and holding them gently but firmly until he struggles to get away. Wait a brief moment or two, then release his paws and give him a cue to sit. He should eventually learn that jumping gets him into an uncomfortable predicament.

Children are major victims of puppy jumping, since puppies view little people as ready targets for jumping up as well as nipping. If your children (or their friends) are unable to dispense jump corrections, you will have to intervene and handle it for them.

Knowing what you should not do is also important to prevention. Never kick or slap your Cavalier (for any reason, not just for jumping) or knock him in the chest with your knee. That maneuver could actually harm your puppy. Vets can tell you stories about puppies who suffered broken bones after getting knocked around when they jumped up.

PUPPY WHINING

Puppies often cry and whine, just as infants and little children do. It's their way of telling us that they're lonely or in need of attention. Your Cavalier puppy will miss his littermates and will feel insecure when he's left alone. You may be out of the house or just in another room, but he'll still feel alone. During these times, the puppy's crate should be his personal comfort station, a place all his own where he can feel safe and secure. Once he learns that being alone is OK and not something to be feared, he'll settle down without crying or objecting. You might want to leave a radio on while he's crated, as the sound of human voices can be soothing and will give the impression that people are around.

Give your puppy a favorite cuddly toy or chew toy to entertain him whenever he's crated. You'll both be happier: the puppy because he is safe in his den and you because he is quiet, safe and not getting into puppy escapades that can wreak havoc in your house or cause him danger.

To make sure that your puppy will always view his crate as a safe and cozy place, never *ever* use the crate for punishment. That's the best way to turn the crate into a negative place that the pup will want to avoid. Sure, you can use the crate for your own peace of mind if your puppy is getting into trouble and needs a timeout. Just don't let him know that! Never scold your puppy then immediately place him into the crate. Count to 10, give him a couple of hugs and maybe a treat, then scoot him into his crate.

It's also important not to make a big fuss when you release him from the crate. That will make getting out of the crate more appealing than being in it, which is just the opposite of what you are trying to achieve.

CHAPTER 11

DOG SPORTS

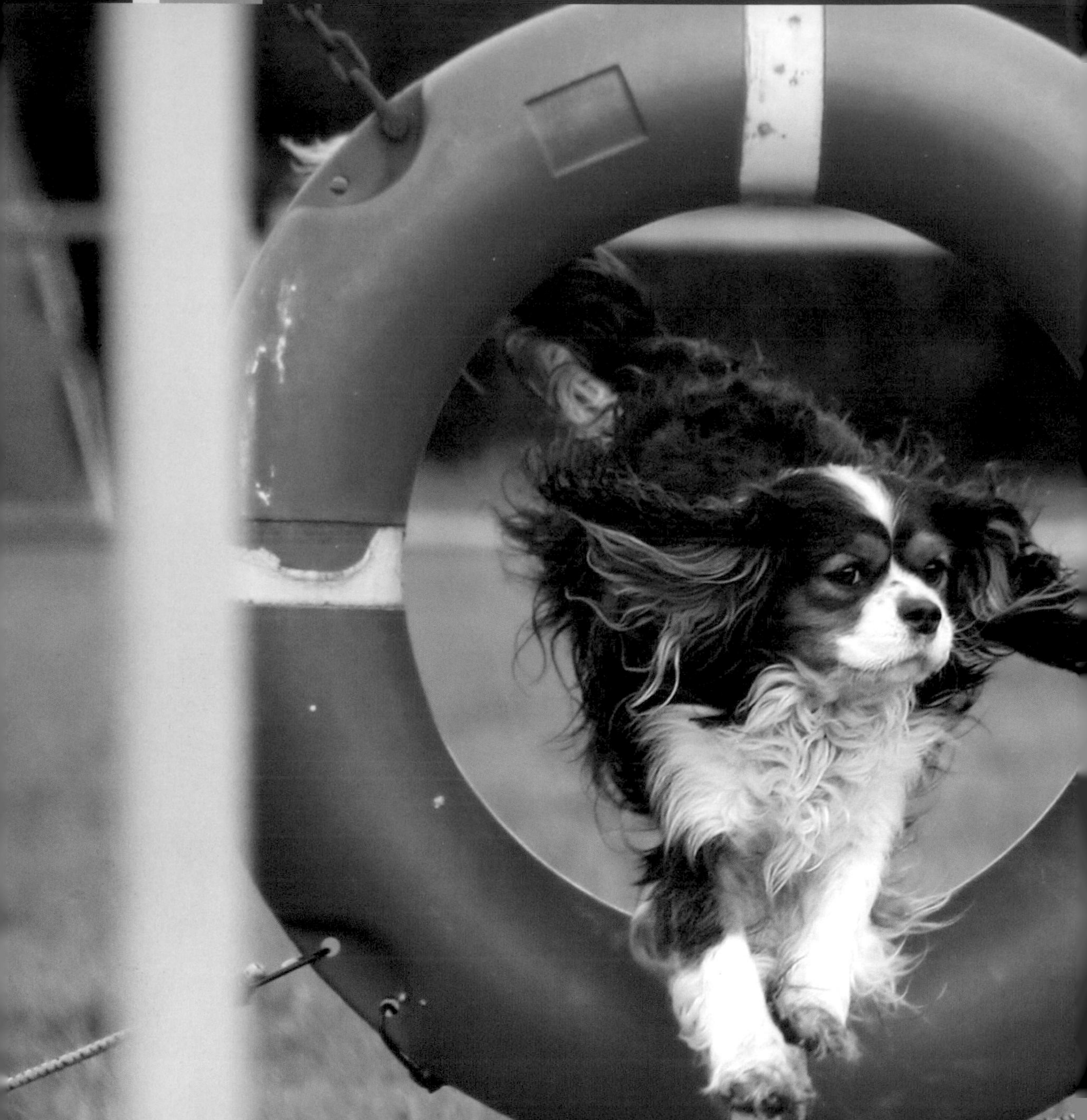

One of the best ways to nurture a cooperative and solid relationship with your Cavalier is to become involved in an activity both of you can enjoy. A bored Cavalier can easily become a troublesome dog.

Deciding what recreation activity you and your Cavalier would enjoy the most takes some consideration. Do you want a sport, such as agility, where you and your dog are both active participants? Would you prefer an activity, such as flyball, where your dog does most of the running? Does something less physical, such as visiting senior citizens, sound more like your cup of tea? Perhaps a brief synopsis of some of the more popular dog-friendly recreations will help you narrow down the choices.

EXERCISE OPTIONS

All Cavaliers need exercise to keep them physically and mentally healthy. An inactive dog is an overweight dog, who will likely suffer joint strain or torn ligaments. Inactive dogs are also prone to mischief and may do anything to relieve their boredom. This often

Did You Know? Canine performance activities provide dogs with a constructive outlet for burning energy. They also provide owners with enjoyable diversions from life's daily demands. Plus, the enhanced communication required in any type of training builds an amazing bond between dog and owner.

leads to behavioral problems, such as chewing or barking. Regular daily exercise, such as walks and play sessions, will keep your Cavalier slim, trim and happy.

Provide your Cav with interactive play that stimulates his mind, as well as his body. It's a good idea to have a daily period of one-on-one play, especially with a puppy or young dog. Continue this type of interaction throughout your dog's life, and you will build a lasting bond. Even senior Cavaliers need the stimulation that activity provides.

If your Cavalier is older or overweight, consult your veterinarian about how much and what type of exercise he needs. Usually, a 10- to 15-minute walk once a day is a good start. As the pounds start to drop off, your dog's energy level will rise, and you can increase the amount of daily exercise.

Whether a dog is trained in the structured environment of a class or alone with his owner at home, there also are many sporting activities that can bring fun and rewards to owner and dog once they have mastered basic training techniques.

AGILITY TRIALS

Agility is a fast-growing canine sport, attracting dogs of all kinds and their equally diverse owners. In agility, the dog, off leash but guided by the handler, runs a course of obstacles including jumps, tunnels, A-frames, elevated boards and more. Basically, the dog must negotiate the obstacles in proper order and style and do it within a set time. The team can strive for high honors, for the titles only or simply for the joy of working together.

Most training facilities require that dogs have some basic obedience training before entering an agility class because your dog must be responsive to you. He must reliably

Competitive dog sports are a great way to keep your active Cavalier entertained.

Weave poles are one of the many obstacles that an agility competitor must master.

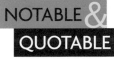

With any small dog, pushing through briars, tall grass and weeds is harder than it is for a big dog. As the handler, we don't really understand how the dog tracks, nor can we see where the track goes, but when the dog is heading down the track, making the turns and finding the articles, it's terrific. — performance competitor, obedience judge and training instructor Sandi Atkinson of Derwood, Md.

Swimming is the safest activity for hotter weather, because the water acts as an external cooling source. Never force your dog into the water; instead, encourage her to enter by throwing in a floatable toy or having her follow you. Start in a calm, shallow area, then work up to deeper water. When playing in a swimming pool, make sure that your dog learns how to exit on her own. Always supervise your Cavalier around any body of water.

refrain from interfering with other dogs and handlers or from running off. It's also important to allow your puppy to mature before undertaking agility jumps and sharp turns because young bones and joints are injured more easily than mature ones.

Multiple organizations sponsor agility titles at all levels, from novice through advanced. The rules, procedures and obstacles vary somewhat among the organizations, so be sure to obtain and read the appropriate rule book before entering your dog in competition. In addition to the American Kennel Club and United Kennel Club, the United States Dog Agility Association and the North American Dog Agility Council also offer agility trials and titles.

The AKC offers Novice Agility, Open Agility, Agility Excellent and Master Agility Excellent titles. To achieve a Master Agility title, a dog must first earn the Agility Excellent title, then earn qualifying scores in the agility excellent class at 10 licensed or member agility trials.

The USDAA offers eight agility titles. An Agility Dog must achieve three clear rounds (no faults) under two different judges in the starters or novice category of competition.

If your Cav isn't into competitive sports, find other ways for her to get the exercise she needs.

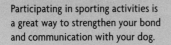

Participating in sporting activities is a great way to strengthen your bond and communication with your dog.

An Advanced Agility Dog has achieved three clear rounds under two different judges in the advanced class. The Masters Agility Dog has demonstrated versatility by achieving three clear rounds under two different judges in the masters standard agility class.

In addition, a dog must receive a qualifying score at the master level in each of the following: Gamblers Competition, to demonstrate proficiency in distance control and handling; Pairs or Team Relay, to demonstrate cooperative team effort and good sportsmanship; Jumping Class, to demonstrate jumping ability and fluid working habit; and Snooker Competition, to further demonstrate a dog and handler's versatility in strategic planning. To earn a Jumpers Master, Gamblers Master, Snooker Master or Relay Master title, a dog must achieve five clear rounds in the appropriate class. A USDAA Agility Dog Champion has earned the MAD, SM, GM, JM and RM titles. The USDAA also recognizes the Agility Top 10 each year.

The USDAA promotes competition by hosting major tournament events, including its Grand Prix of Dog Agility championships, the Dog Agility Masters Team Pentathlon Championship promotes agility as a team sport and the Dog Agility Steeplechase championship focuses on speed in performance. Dogs must be registered with the USDAA in order to compete in this organization's events.

The USDAA also offers programs for older dogs and younger handlers. The Veterans Program is for dogs 7 years of age or older. The Junior Handler Program is for handlers up to 18 years of age and is designed to encourage young people to participate in dog agility as a fun, recreational family sport.

The North American Dog Agility Council offers certificates of achievement for the regular, jumpers and gamblers classes. The purpose of the regular agility class is to demonstrate the handler-and-dog team's ability to perform all of the agility obstacles safely and at a moderate rate of speed. At the open level, the goal is to test the handler-and-dog team's ability to perform the obstacles more quickly and with more directional and distance control and obstacle discrimination.

At the elite level, more complex handler strategies are tested, with the dog moving at a brisk pace. The dog may be entered in the standard, veterans or junior handlers divisions. In all divisions, certification in the regular agility classes will require three qualifying rounds under at least two different judges. The NADAC also awards an Agility Trial Champion title.

TRACKING

The sport of tracking, as outlined by the AKC, calls for a dog to locate and steadily follow a specific human scent trail that has the distance, age, number of turns and "lost" articles required for that competition level. Titles can be earned based on the type of land covered, either rural, natural terrain or citified surfaces such as pavement and gravel.

Though urban tracking promises to become more popular, most takes place over rural ground. Dogs must work through various types of vegetation, weather conditions, insects, other animal scents and chance encounters with various critters. Since the handler follows at the end of the lead, this tends to be a sport for outdoors lovers.

The breed's usual keenness for hunting and affinity for food blend well in training, as most people initially place treats in their footsteps to keep the dog's head down and create a pleasant association with scenting. Treats are gradually reduced until the dog

Cavaliers can be enthusiastic competitors in conformation; they are steady and willing workers in obedience, and they excel in agility, all the while waving their plumed tails. They are often very intuitive about people and know just how to approach an individual, so they make excellent therapy dogs.

— breeder and American Kennel Club Cavalier provisional judge Joanne Nash of Los Altos Hills, California

Before jumping into any activity, schedule a veterinary examination to check your Cavalier for possible health problems. Eye disorders and improperly formed joints are both prevalent in dogs. Mitral valve disease, a serious heart condition that often requires medication, is common in the Cavalier and should be ruled out before beginning training in any physically demanding sport.

can complete a track without such incentives, instead of receiving praise from the handler.

Despite the hardships that go along with tracking, this sport ranks as a frequent favorite among trainers. Most people love the early morning outings, time spent exploring the outdoors and opportunity to watch their dogs master an inherent ability far superior to our own.

Many books and videos give step-by-step instructions for teaching your dog to track, making it one of the easier sports to do on your own. However, nothing substitutes for experienced instruction. Contact your nearest training club to see if any members track, or check the AKC's website for listings of clubs that hold tracking tests.

OBEDIENCE TRIALS

Obedience trials in the United States trace back to the early 1930s, when organized obedience training was developed to demonstrate how well dogs and their owners could work together. Helen Whitehouse Walker, a Standard Poodle fancier, pioneered obedience trials after she modeled a series of exercises after the Associated Sheep, Police and Army Dog Society of Great Britain. Since Walker initiated the first trials, competitive

obedience has grown by leaps and bounds, and today more than 2,000 trials are held in the United States every year, with more than 100,000 dogs competing. Any registered AKC or UKC dog can enter an obedience trial for the club in which he's registered, regardless of conformational disqualifications or spaying/neutering.

Obedience trials are divided into three levels of progressive difficulty. At the first level, Novice, the dogs compete for the title of Companion Dog; at the intermediate level, Open, dogs compete for a Companion Dog Excellent title; and at the Advanced level, dogs compete for a Utility Dog title. Classes are subdivided into "A" (for beginners) and "B" (for more experienced handlers). A perfect score at any level is 200, and a dog must score 170 or better to earn a "leg," three of which are needed to earn the title.

To earn points, a dog must score more than 50 percent of the available points in each exercise; the points range is from 20 to 40.

Once a dog has earned the Utility Dog title, he can compete with other proven obedience dogs for the coveted title of Utility Dog Excellent, which requires that the dog win "legs" in 10 shows. In 1977, the AKC established the title of Obedience Trial Champion. Utility Dogs who earn legs in Open B and Utility B earn points toward their Obedience Trial Champion title. To become an OTCh., a dog needs to earn 100 points, which requires three first-place wins in Open B and Utility B under three different judges.

Obedience trials show off your skills in working with your dog. It's among the most challenging canine sports.

The Grand Prix of obedience trials, the AKC National Obedience Invitational, gives qualifying Utility Dogs the chance to win the newest and highest title: National Obedience Champion. Only the top 25 ranked obedience dogs, plus any dog ranked in the top three in his breed, are allowed to compete.

RALLY BEHIND RALLY

Rally is a sport that combines competition obedience with elements of agility, but it is less demanding than either activity. Rally was designed with the average dog owner in mind and is easier than many other sporting activities.

At a rally event, dogs and handlers are asked to move through 10 to 20 different stations, depending on the level of competition. The stations are marked by numbered signs, which tell the handler the exercise to be performed. The exercises vary from making different types of turns to changing pace.

Dogs can earn rally titles as they get better at the sport and move through the different levels. The titles to strive for are Rally

SMART TIP!

In addition to performance activities, noncompetitive pastimes, such as walking, hiking and playing provide equally pleasurable ways to spend time with your Cavalier. However, because dogs overheat rather easily, limit walking to times when the temperature will stay below 80 degrees. Even then, for longer hikes it's advisable to take along a doggie carrying pack in case your Cavalier gets tired, as well as water and snacks for you both.

Novice, Rally Advanced, Rally Excellent and Rally Advanced Excellent.

To get your Cavalier puppy prepared to enter a rally competition, focus on teaching him basic obedience, for starters. Your dog must know the five basic obedience cues — sit, down, stay, come and heel — and perform them well. Next, you can enroll your dog in a rally class. Although he must be

Agility is an easier sport to start your dog in. As she earns her event titles, you can introduce her to other sports to continue to challenge her abilities.

There are so many ways to have fun with your dog. Keep trying new things until you find an activity you both enjoy.

at least 6 months of age to compete in rally, you can start training long before his 6-month birthday.

FUN WITH FLYBALL

Flyball is a team sport for dogs that was invented in California by a group of dog trainers in the late 1970s. It is a fun sport that dogs of any breed or mixture can compete in and is the only dog competition that is a team event. Flyball gives dogs lots of exercise and the training works their minds as well as their bodies.

This canine relay race consists of four straight-line hurdles set at a height appropriate for the shortest member of the four-dog team. Beyond these jumps sits a box that ejects a tennis ball whenever the release lever is hit. The object is for each dog to clear the hurdles, push the release, catch the ejected tennis ball and repeat its path back to the waiting handler, which allows the next dog in line to be released. The North American Flyball Association maintains the breed statistics and awards titles.

Not surprisingly, the ideal flyball dog loves to fetch and has a special affinity for

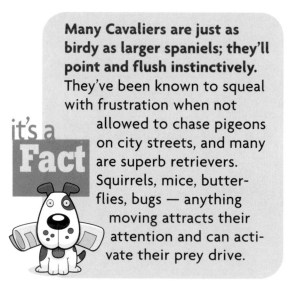

Many Cavaliers are just as birdy as larger spaniels; they'll point and flush instinctively. They've been known to squeal with frustration when not allowed to chase pigeons on city streets, and many are superb retrievers. Squirrels, mice, butterflies, bugs — anything moving attracts their attention and can activate their prey drive.

tennis balls. Cavaliers frequently love retrieving, but not every dog will have the tenacity to consistently jump at the speeds necessary for flyball. Those that do will find an energy-burning good time that, like agility, requires participants to be physically fit. Many training clubs have incorporated flyball into their curriculums. Contact the NAFA for advice on finding or starting a flyball group in your area.

SHOW DOGS

When you purchase your Cavalier puppy, make it clear to the breeder whether you want one just as a lovable companion and pet, or if you hope to purchase a Cavalier with show prospects. No reputable breeder will sell you a puppy and tell you that he will definitely be show *quality* because so much can change during the early months of a puppy's development. If you do plan to show, what you hopefully will have acquired is a puppy with show *potential*.

To the novice, exhibiting a Cavalier in the ring may look easy, but it takes a lot of hard work and devotion to win any show — be it a local one or the annual Westminster Kennel Club Dog Show in New York City — not to mention a fair amount of luck, too!

The first concept that the canine novice learns when watching a dog show is that each dog first competes against members of his own breed. Once the judge has selected the best dog in each breed (Best of Breed) the chosen dog will compete with other dogs in his group. Finally, the dogs chosen first in each group will compete for the Best in Show title.

The second thing to understand is that the dogs aren't actually compared against one another. Each dog is compared against the breed standard, the written description of the ideal dog approved by the AKC.

While some early breed standards were based on specific dogs who were famous or popular, many dedicated enthusiasts say that a perfect specimen as described in the standard has never walked into a show ring, has never been bred and, to the woe of dog breeders around the globe, does not exist. Breeders attempt to get as close to this ideal as possible with every litter, but theoretically the "perfect" dog is so elusive that it is impossible. (Even if the perfect dog was born, breeders and judges probably would never agree that he was perfect!)

If you are interested in exploring the world of conformation, your best bet is to join your local breed club or the national (or parent) club, the American Cavalier King Charles Spaniel Club. These clubs often host regional and national specialties, shows only for Cavalier, which can include conformation as well as obedience and field trials. Even if you have no intention of competing with your Cavalier, a specialty is like a festival for lovers of the breed who congregate to share their favorite topic: the Cavalier! Clubs also send out newsletters, and some organize training days and seminars providing owners the opportunity to learn more about their chosen breed. To locate the breed club closest to you, contact the AKC, which furnishes the rules and regulations for all of these events, plus general dog registration and other basic requirements of dog ownership.

Although a toy breed, Cavalier King Charles Spaniels are also natural pointers and retrievers. Any moving object can activate their prey drive.

MUSICAL FREESTYLE

A stunning combination of obedience, tricks and dance, freestyle is the perfect venue for those possessing an artistic flair. Set within a large, open ring, each handler-and-dog pair performs a personally choreographed routine in rhythm to their choice of music. A typical presentation might find a dog weaving between the handler's legs as he or she is walking, spinning in place, doing leg kicks and other imaginative moves. Creative handler costumes and fancy dog collars often complete the picture.

Most participants agree that dogs display preferences in music, responding happily to tunes they like while ignoring those they don't. If you're worried about your own questionable dance skills, keep in mind that the self-choreography allows you to focus on your team's special talents.

Find the Fred Astaire in your Cavalier King Charles Spaniel at a local training facility or with a private trainer. Alternatively, contact the sport's host organizations, the Canine Freestyle Federation and the World Canine Freestyle Organization, for information about getting your dog's start in this fun activity. See the Resources chapter on page 162 for more information.

CHAPTER 12

THE GOLDEN

Before you know it, seven or eight years will fly by, and you'll realize that your sweet Cavalier has a few gray hairs in his muzzle and he's moving a little slower than he used to. Faster than you ever thought possible, your dog is in his senior years. In most cases, caring for your senior Cavalier won't be any different from what you've always done, but you should be aware of the challenges a senior dog faces.

There is no definitive age that makes your Cavalier a senior. However, most veterinarians consider a dog to be a senior when he reaches 75 percent of his breed's average lifespan. So Cavaliers are generally considered seniors at around 7 years old. Remember that Cavaliers are individuals, so when and how each dog will age will vary. As always, you are your dog's best health advocate, so it's important to monitor his health especially as he gets older.

SIGNS OF AGING

You might begin to notice a number of small changes in your Cavalier's behavior. Some general signs of aging include:
◆ graying around the muzzle, face and eyes
◆ taking longer to stand up from a prone position
◆ more interest in napping and laying on the couch than in playing
◆ hair loss
◆ hearing problems
◆ dental disease

These are just a few telltale signs of aging. However, it's important to note that any time you see a physical or behavioral change in your dog, no matter what his age, you should consult your veterinarian.

Also, you shouldn't assume that pain or difficulty moving is just a natural part of the aging process for your dog. There are many treatments available that can help your dog with the health issues he'll face in old age.

Along with physical changes, you may begin to notice behavioral changes as well. There are many reasons why you may see a change in your Cav's behavior. Sometimes a dog's apparent confusion is caused by a physical issue like diminished sight or hearing. If his confusion causes him to be afraid, he may act aggressively or defensively. He may sleep more frequently because his daily walks, though shorter now, tire him out. He may begin to experience separation anxiety or, conversely, become less interested in your petting and attention. If you notice a change in your Cavalier's behavior, consult your veterinarian right away so you can find out what's affecting your Cavalier's normally pleasant temperament.

COMMON SENIOR AILMENTS

Arthritis: Degenerative joint disease, often referred to as arthritis, is common in elderly dogs. A lifetime of wear and tear on joints eventually takes its toll and results in stiffness and difficulty in getting around. As dogs live longer and healthier lives, it is natural that they should eventually feel some of the effects of aging. Maintaining a healthy weight throughout life may lessen the severity. If your pet was unfortunate enough to inherit hip dysplasia, osteochondrosis dissecans or any of the other developmental orthopedic diseases, battling the onset of degenerative joint disease is a longstanding goal. There are now many effective remedies for managing degenerative joint disease and a number of remarkable surgeries as well.

Doggie Alzheimer: Cognitive dysfunction shares much in common with senility

and Alzheimer's disease, and dogs are not immune. Dogs can become confused and/or disoriented, have accidents in the house, have abnormal sleep patterns and interact differently with their owners. Be heartened by the fact that, in some ways, there are more treatment options for dogs with cognitive dysfunction than for people with similar conditions. There is good evidence that continued stimulation in the form of games, play, training and exercise can help to maintain cognitive function. Medications and antioxidant-fortified senior diets have shown to be beneficial, but check with your veterinarian about the best option for your aging Cavalier.

Cancer: Almost all of the cancers seen in people are also seen in pets. If your dog is getting regular physical examinations, cancers are often detected early. There are a variety of cancer therapies available today, and many pets continue to live happy lives with appropriate treatment.

Don't let this summary of problems associated with aging alarm you. Your dog most likely won't fall apart or become more difficult as he ages. Many hardy dogs remain active and alert well into old age. However, it can be frustrating and heartbreaking for owners to see their beloved dogs change physically and temperamentally. Just know that he's still your same Cavalier despite any changes and

Dogs can suffer from many of the same ailments as we do in old age, such as cancer, arthritis and dementia.

that he still loves you and appreciates your care, which he needs now more than ever.

CARING FOR YOUR SENIOR DOG

Every dog is an individual in terms of aging. Your dog might reach the estimated senior age for his breed and show no signs of slowing down. However, even if he shows no outward signs of aging, he should begin a senior-care program once he reaches 7 or 8 years old. He may not show it, but he's not a pup anymore! By providing extra attention to his veterinary care at this age, you will be practicing good preventive medicine, ensuring that the rest of your dog's life will be as long, active, happy and healthy as possible. If you do notice indications of aging, such as graying and/or changes in sleeping, eating or elimination habits, this is a sign to set up a visit with your vet right away to make sure that these changes aren't related to any health problems.

To start, senior dogs should visit the vet twice yearly for exams, routine tests and overall evaluations. Many veterinarians have special screening programs especially for senior dogs that can include a thorough physical exam; blood test to determine a complete blood count; serum biochemistry test, which screens for liver, kidney and blood problems, as well as cancer; urinalysis; and dental exams. These tests can determine whether your dog has any health problems; the results also establish a baseline for your pet against which future test results can be compared.

In addition to these tests, your vet may suggest additional testing, including an EKG, tests for glaucoma and other problems of the eyes, chest X-rays, screening for tumors, a blood pressure test, a test for thyroid function, and screening for parasites and a reassessment of his preventive program. Your vet also will ask you questions about your dog's diet and activity level, what you feed and the amounts that you feed. This information, along with his evaluation of the dog's overall condition, will enable him to suggest proper dietary changes, if needed.

This may seem like quite a work-up for your pet, but older dogs need more frequent attention so that any health problems can be detected as early as possible. Serious conditions like kidney disease, heart disease and cancer may not present outward symptoms, or the problem may go undetected if owners just mistake the symptoms as just part of the aging process.

Aside from the extra veterinary care, there is a lot you can do at home to keep your older dog happy and comfortable. Your dog's diet is an important factor. If his appetite decreases, he won't be getting the nutrients he needs. He'll also lose weight, which is unhealthy for a dog at a proper weight. An older dog's metabolism is slower, and he usually exercises less, but he shouldn't be allowed to become obese. Obesity in an older dog is especially risky because extra pounds mean added stress on the body,

it's a **Fact**

Not all senior dogs become overweight. Some Cavaliers maintain a near-optimal body condition well into their senior years. A surprising number of senior dogs actually lose weight as they age. This weight loss may be caused by decreased food intake, which often occurs with chronic health problems — dental disorders, diabetes, cancer, heart or kidney disease, and many others.

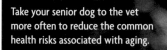
Take your senior dog to the vet more often to reduce the common health risks associated with aging.

increasing his vulnerability to heart disease. The extra pounds also make it more difficult for the dog to move around.

Discuss any age-related feeding changes beforehand with your vet. For a dog who has lost interest in food, try some different types of food until you find something new that your dog likes. For an obese dog, a weight-control formula or reduced food portions may be advised, along with exercise appropriate to his physical condition and energy level.

As for exercise, the senior dog shouldn't be allowed to become a couch potato despite his old age. He may not be able to handle the morning run, long walks and vigorous games of fetch, but he still needs to get up and get moving. Keep up with your daily walks, but keep the distances shorter and let your dog set the pace. If he gets to the point where he's not up for walks, let him stroll around the yard. Some dogs remain very active in their senior years, so changes to your dog's exercise program should be based on what he's capable of doing. Don't worry; your Cavalier will let you know when it's time to rest.

Keep up with your regular grooming routine. Be extra diligent about checking your dog's skin and coat for problems. Older dogs can experience thinning coats as part of the normal aging process, but they can also lose hair as a result of medical problems. Some thinning is normal, but patches of baldness or the loss of significant amounts of hair aren't.

Hopefully, you've been regularly brush your dog's teeth throughout his life. Healthy teeth directly affect overall good health. We already know that bacteria from gum infections can enter the dog's body through the damaged gums and travel to the organs. At a stage in life when his organs don't function as well as they used to, you don't want anything to put additional strain on them. Clean teeth also contribute to a healthy immune system. Offering dental-type chews in addition to brushing his teeth can help, as they remove plaque and tartar when the dog chews.

Along with the same good care you've given him all his life, pay a little extra attention to your dog in his senior years and keep up with twice-yearly trips to the vet. The sooner a problem is uncovered, the greater the chances of a full recovery.

SAYING GOODBYE

While you can help your dog live as long a life as possible, you can't help him live forever. A dog's lifespan is short when compared to that of a human, so it is inevitable that pet owners will experience loss. To many, losing a beloved dog is like losing a family member. Our dogs are part of our everyday lives; they are our true loyal friends and always seem to know when it's time to comfort us, to celebrate with us or to just provide the company of a caring friend. Even when we know that our dogs are nearing their final days, we can never quite prepare for their absence.

Many dogs live out long lives and simply die of old age. Others unfortunately are taken

The ability to metabolize protein decreases with age; so even if they're healthy, seniors need up to 50 percent more protein than younger adults. Inadequate protein intake can cause muscle degeneration, general weakness and immune system impairment. To prevent protein deficiencies, most senior foods now contain as much protein as puppy foods.

it's a **Fact**

suddenly by illness or accident, and still others find their senior years compromised by disease and physical problems. In some of these cases, owners find themselves having to make difficult decisions.

Euthanasia: When the end comes for a beloved pet, it is a very difficult time for his owners. This time is made even more difficult when the owners are faced with making a choice regarding euthanasia, more commonly known as having a very sick or very aged dog put to sleep or put down.

Euthanasia is defined as the act of ending the life of an individual suffering from a terminal illness or an incurable condition; the word "euthanasia" has its roots in Greek, meaning "good death." Euthanasia is usually accomplished by injection or other medical means that do not cause pain to the patient.

Veterinary euthanasia means that a pet is injected with a concentrated dose of anesthesia, causing unconsciousness within a few seconds and death soon after. This process is painless for the dog; the only discomfort he may feel is the prick of the needle, the same as he would with any other injection.

The decision of whether or not to euthanize is undoubtedly the most difficult that owners have to make regarding their pets.

It's a very emotional decision, yet it requires clear thinking, discussion with the vet and, of course, discussion with all family members. During this time, owners will experience many different feelings: guilt, sadness and possibly anger at having to make this type of decision. Many times, it is difficult to actually come to a decision, thinking that maybe the dog will miraculously recover or that maybe he will succumb to his illness, making the decision no longer necessary.

When faced with the decision to euthanize, you must take many things into consideration; first and foremost, what is best for your dog? Hopefully you have a good relationship with a vet whose medical opinion you trust and with whom you can discuss your decision openly and honestly. Remember that good vets are animal lovers, too, and they want the best for their patients. Your vet should talk to you about your dog's condition and the reality of what the rest of his days will be like: Will he be able to live out his days relatively comfortably or will the rest of his life be filled with pain? Many people believe that euthanasia is the way to mercifully end a pet's suffering.

You have many factors to consider. It's best to include all members of the family in each step of the decision-making process. Some of the things to think about include the current quality of your Cavalier's life, whether he is constantly ill and/or in pain, whether there are things you can do to give him a comfortable life even if he has an incurable condition, whether you've explored all treatment options, whether you've discussed the behavioral aspects of your pet's problems with an expert, and whether you've thoroughly discussed with the veterinarian your Cavalier's prognosis and the likelihood of him enjoying a normal life ever again.

Of course, the aforementioned considerations present just some of the things that you will need to think about. You will have many questions and concerns of your own. Never feel pressured; take time to make a decision with which you will be comfortable.

If you've come to the decision that euthanasia is the right choice for your pet, there are a few further, equally heartbreaking, choices to make. Do you or another family member want to be present with your dog during the procedure? How will you say goodbye? Should you arrange for someone to accompany you to the vet for support so that you don't have to drive in a state of grief? Again, your emotions will be running

A good vet will have your senior dog's quality of life in mind while making recommendations about her continued care.

high during this very difficult time, so think through your decisions clearly and rely on the support of family and friends.

The Grieving Process: Our pets are such big parts of our lives that we naturally grieve for them when they pass away. To some, the loss of a pet affects them the same way the loss of a friend or family member would; to many, dogs are friends and family members.

Grieving over your pet is normal; in fact, it is necessary. The grieving process is the same, whether for a human or a pet. During this time you may want to seek the support of other animal lovers who have experienced the same thing, as they are sure to understand your feelings, offer a sympathetic ear and offer kind advice. People without pets may not grasp the true scope of what you are going through, but hopefully they'll still acknowledge your pain and offer their condolences. Your response to your pet's death and your mourning are very personal, and you don't have to justify your feelings to anyone. Anyone who doesn't appreciate the value of a beloved pet obviously hasn't been blessed with the fulfillment that a pet's companionship brings.

That being said, many people will completely understand your grief. This includes people who knew your pet well (like friends, your vet or your groomer), as well as other pet lovers (maybe in a support group or pet-bereavement website). There are many places online where pet lovers gather to share their grief, as well as their cherished memories. You likely also will be able to find bereavement counselors or discussion groups that meet in your area. You might also find comfort in your religious beliefs and can seek the support of clergy members.

Despite your sadness, you can find happiness in the times that you and your pet spent together. Your memories will always remind you of how your life was enriched by your Cavalier King Charles Spaniel.

WHAT'S NEXT

Of course, following the death of a beloved pet, each person goes through a period of mourning. As time goes on and you become more accepting of the fact that your pet has passed on, your thoughts may turn to how to fill the void that your cherished companion has left behind. For some, dealing with and acceptance of a pet's death takes longer than others. Everyone grieves differently, so your should take the time that your need to start feeling better. A source of comfort for many, when they are ready, is to add a new pet to the home, while other people feel as if they are betraying their departed friends by doing so. As time passes, you will decide how best to move on, so don't feel the need to rush into anything before you are absolutely ready. Allow yourself the time that you need to mourn and to heal.

If you decide that you'd like to add a new pet to the household, don't feel guilty. You aren't trying to replace your Cavalier, nor should you; giving a new puppy or adult dog a new home is the most sincere way to honor the memory of your beloved pet. No pet will ever replace another, but a new dog will create new happiness and new memories.

Do you want a new puppy? Chances are, if your aging dog had battled with illness, you had put much time and effort into his care. Puppies require just as much time and effort: Are you ready to start over? Many owners enjoy the aspect of raising a dog from youth and the special dog/owner bond that results. If you stayed in contact with your dog's breeder throughout the dog's life, you have a good place to begin your puppy search.

Another wonderful option is to look into adopting an adult dog from a rescue. There are many wonderful dogs out there that end up homeless because of their former owners' bad decision-making. In thinking of the special relationship that you shared with your dog, maybe you'd like to give one of these deserving dogs a second chance?

If you'd like another Cavalier, start by contacting the breeder you originally purchased your Cavalier from or the American Cavalier King Charles Spaniel Club. You may decide on another breed to avoid comparison with your departed friend, or you may decide to take a trip to your local animal shelter to see whether you hit it off with one of the dogs there.

If you aren't ready for a new dog, there are other ways that you can enjoy canine companionship. Perhaps you'd like to become involved at your local shelter or with a breed rescue. That way, you can still spend time with dogs, and it will be fulfilling for you to know that you are helping them. You may even decide to provide a foster home for adoptable dogs.

However you decide to deal with your grief, keep your memories close to you. Your dog may no longer be with you, but you will always have the happiness of your wonderful years together. Hopefully, those memories will make you a dog lover for life.

Cavaliers can live fulfilling lives throughout their senior years. Keep this commitment in mind as you're considering bringing one into your home and family.

Smart owners can find out more information about this popular and fascinating breed by contacting the following organizations. They will be glad to help you dig deeper into the world of Cavs, and you won't even have to beg!

Academy of Veterinary Homeopathy: Founded in 1995, the AVH is comprised of veterinarians who share the common desire to restore true health to their patients through the use of homeopathic treatment. www.theavh.org

American Animal Hospital Association: The AAHA accredits small-animal hospitals throughout the United States and Canada with approximately 6,000 practice teams and 40,000 car providers. www.healthypet.com

American Cavalier King Charles Spaniel Club: This is the AKC's parent club and the main club for the Cavalier King Charles Spaniel in the United States. This is a great organization to find out more about Cavalier King Charles Spaniels, breeder referrals and more. www.ackcsc.org

American Dog Owners Association: The ADOA is the nation's oldest and largest member-based organization representing dog owners for responsible dog ownership. www.adoa.org

it's a **Fact**

The American Kennel Club was established in 1884. It is America's oldest kennel club. The United Kennel Club is the second oldest in the United States. It began registering dogs in 1898.

American Holistic Veterinary Medical Association: The AHVMA explores and supports alternative and complementary approaches to veterinary healthcare and is dedicated to integrating all aspects of animal wellness in a socially and environmentally responsible manner. www.ahvma.org

American Humane Association: Founded in 1877, the AHA is a nonprofit membership organization dedicated to protecting children and animals. www.americanhumane.org

American Kennel Club: The AKC website offers information and links to sporting programs, member clubs and all things dog. www.akc.org

American Kennel Club Canine Health Foundation: This foundation is the world's largest nonprofit funder of exclusively canine research. www.akcchf.org

American Society for the Prevention of Cruelty to Animals: The ASPCA was the first humane organization in the Western Hemisphere. Its mission is "to provide effective means for the prevention of cruelty to animals throughout the United States." www.aspca.org

American Veterinary Medical Association: This nonprofit represents more than 80,000 vets working in private and corporate practice, government, industry, academia and uniformed services. www.avma.org

Association of American Feed Control Officials: The AAFCO develops and implements uniform and equitable laws, regulations, standards and enforcement policies for regulating the manufacture, distribution and sale of animal feeds, which results in safe, effective and useful feeds. www.aafco.org

Association of Pet Dog Trainers: The APDT is a professional organization of individual dog trainers who are committed to becoming better trainers through education. www.apdt.com

Canadian Kennel Club: Our northern neighbor's oldest kennel club is similar to the AKC in the States. www.ckc.ca

Canine Performance Events: Sports help keep dogs active. www.k9cpe.com

Delta Society: This organization offers animal assistance to people in need. www.deltasociety.org

Dog Scouts of America: Take your dog to camp. www.dogscouts.com

Fédération Cynologique Internationale: The World Canine Organization includes 84 members and contract partners (one member per country), all who issue their own pedigrees and train their own judges. www.fci.be

Love on a Leash: This is a therapy dog organization. Your sweet dog has a lot of love to give others. www.loveonaleash.org

National Association of Professional Pet Sitters: When you will be away for a while, hire someone to watch and entertain your dog. www.petsitters.org

North American Dog Agility Council: This agility organization's website provides links to clubs, obedience trainers and agility trainers in the United States and Canada. www.nadac.com

Pet Care Services Association: This nonprofit trade association includes nearly 3,000 pet-care service businesses in the United States and around the world. www.petcareservices.org

Pet Sitters International: This organization's mission is to educate professional pet sitters and to promote, support and recognize excellence in pet sitting. www.petsit.com

SPAY/USA: This nationwide spay/neuter network and referral service, from the North Shore Animal League America, has more than 1,000 sterilization programs and clinics nationwide with more than 7,000 veterinarians. www.spayusa.org

Teacup Dogs Agility Association: The Cavalier certainly fits this association's purpose: "to provide a competitive venue for dogs of small stature without regard to breed or pedigree." http://teacupagility.com

Therapy Dogs International: Find more therapy dog info here: www.tdi-dog.org

United Kennel Club: The UKC offers several of the events offered by the AKC, including agility, conformation and obedience. In addition, the UKC offers competitions in hunting and dog sport (companion and protective events). www.ukcdogs.com

United States Dog Agility Association: The USDAA has info on training, clubs and events in the United States, Canada, Mexico and overseas. www.usdaa.com

World Canine Freestyle Organization: This association organizes competitions in the fun new sport of dog dancing. www.worldcaninefreestyle.org

OUT AND ABOUT

Cavalier King Charles Spaniels make wonderful travel companions, and just about any place you want to go your Cavalier will be happy to follow. They are excellent travelers and easily adapt to cars, airplanes and boats, as long as you plan ahead.

Car Travel: Like everything else, it's a good idea to introduce your Cavalier to car rides when he's a puppy. Begin desensitizing your dog to travel as a pup so that it's something he's used to. Some dogs do suffer from motion sickness, but with practice, they can get used to being in the car. Other dogs take to the car without a moment's hesitation. If you have a dog with a severe case of motion sickness, your veterinarian may prescribe medication to help alleviate the problem.

Start taking your puppy on short trips, just around the block to start. If he's fine with short trips, lengthen your rides a little at a time. Start to take him on your errands or just for drives around town. By this time, it will be easy to tell whether your dog is a born traveler or if he'd prefer to stay at home when you are on the road.

Of course, safety is a concern for dogs in the car. First, your Cav must travel securely, not left loose to roam around the car where he could be injured or distract the driver. All dogs should travel in crates, which can be the same crate yours uses in the home. Other options include a car harness (like a seat belt for dogs) and partitioning the back of the car with a gate made for this purpose.

There are a couple of very important reasons why it's never a good idea to leave your dog alone in the car. First, many dogs have died from the heat inside closed cars. A closed car is like an oven, and a cracked window won't offer relief. A study by the Stanford University School of Medicine demonstrated that even with temperatures as low as 72 degrees, a car's interior temperature can heat up to 40 degrees higher than the outside temperature. The study also found that 80 percent of the heat increase happens within the first 30 minutes. So when it's only 72 degrees outside, your dog is in danger of suffering from heatstroke as the temperature inside the car climbs to more than 100 degrees. A dog left alone in a car is also an easy target for thieves, and many purebred dogs have been stolen from unattended vehicles.

Don't risk the health and safety of your dog by leaving him alone in a car. Either leave your precious pooch safe at home or make sure someone else stays in the car with him.

For longer road trips, planning is essential when taking your Cavalier along. You'll need to pack essentials for him just like you do for the rest of the family. Make sure your dog is wearing a collar with current ID tags. Also, if your Cavalier is microchipped, make sure the company he is registered with has all your current contact information.

In addition, you'll need to pack:

- ✔ a crate
- ✔ a leash
- ✔ food and water bowls
- ✔ cleanup material for potty breaks
- ✔ food and water
- ✔ favorite toys
- ✔ current medications (if applicable)
- ✔ a brush/comb
- ✔ flea and tick prevention
- ✔ heartworm prevention (if applicable)
- ✔ towels
- ✔ a urine/stain remover

It's also a good idea to find out where an emergency veterinarian is located in the areas you'll be traveling through or at your final destination. Make sure you have the veterinarian's phone number and directions to the office. The last thing you want to be doing during an emergency is looking for a vet clinic in an unfamiliar location. Having this information at your fingertips will save time during an emergency.

When you arrive at your destination, take a few precautions. One of the most important is to check for the presence of rat poison. Many hotels will place a block of rat poison under the radiator, air conditioning unit, bed or refrigerator. Rat poison is deadly, but it has a wonderful smell, and a dog will gobble it up without a second thought. Before you let your dog roam freely in either a hotel room or even at a friend or relative's house, first check for anything poisonous that your dog could get into. People who don't live with dogs may not realize that certain plants and foods are hazardous to a dog's health. It's up to you to ask them questions and to search the premises before you let your dog roam free.

Airline Travel: Taking a trip by air doesn't mean that your dog can't accompany you, it just means that you will have to be informed and prepared. The majority of dogs travel as checked cargo; only the smallest of breeds are allowed in the cabins with their owners. Your Cavalier should be small enough to travel with you in the cabin. Airlines do charge a fee for your dog to travel in the cabin or cargo area.

If you travel with your dog in the cabin, you will need an airline-approved soft travel carrier. This soft carrier is a comfortable space for your dog to lie under the seat while on an airplane. You'll also need to take your dog to the veterinarian before you travel, to obtain a health certificate and proof of rabies vaccination.

You will need to show this information at the airline ticket counter when checking in.

Also keep in mind that many airlines will only allow a certain number of dogs in the cabin per flight; so when you make an airline reservation, make sure to tell them that you want to fly with your dog in the cabin. Remember, too, that some airlines do not allow dogs in their cabins; so check with the airline in advance when you make your reservation.

Flying with your dog in the cabin is a privilege, not a right. So be courteous and considerate at the airport. While many people will be happy to see your Cavalier, not everyone is a dog lover. Also the rules vary from airport to airport about when your dog needs to be in his travel carrier. In general, once you go through security, they prefer that dogs be in their carriers. Yes, your cuddly pooch must go through security, so be prepared.

Traveling with your Cav can be a lot of fun. Just be sure to stay in areas where dogs are allowed and keep yours on a leash.

If you can't take your Cavalier in cabin with you for some reason, he will need to travel through the cargo department of your airline. In cargo, your dog must travel in a sturdy airline-approved travel crate appropriate to his size so that he will be safe and comfortable during the flight. If the crate that you use at home doesn't meet the airline's specifications, you can purchase one from the airline or from your pet-supply store (making sure it is labeled as "airline-approved").

It's best to have the crate in advance of your trip to give your Cavalier King Charles Spaniel time to get accustomed to it. You can put a familiar blanket and a favorite toy or two in the crate with the dog to make him feel at home and to keep him occupied. The crate should be lined with absorbent material for the trip, with bowls for food and water attached to the outside of the crate. The crate must be labeled with your contact information, feeding instructions and a statement asserting that the dog was fed within a certain time frame of arrival at the airport (check with your airline). Again, you will also have to provide proof of current vaccinations.

Advance planning is the key to smooth sailing in the skies. Make your reservations well ahead of time and know what restrictions your airline imposes: no travel during certain months, refusal of certain breeds, restrictions on certain destinations, etc. In spite of all of these variables, major carriers have much experience with transporting animals, so have a safe flight!

DOG-FRIENDLY DESTINATIONS

When planning vacations, a question that often arises is, "Who will watch the dog?" More and more families, however, are answering that question with, "We will!"

With the rise in dog-friendly places to visit, the number of families who bring their dogs along on vacation is on the rise. A search online for dog-friendly vacation spots will turn up many choices, as well as resources for owners of canine travelers. Ask others for suggestions: your veterinarian, your breeder, other dog owners, breed club members, people at the local doggie day care. You might also visit your local bookstore's travel section. There you'll find many books dedicated to dog-friendly destination spots around the country.

When you travel with your dog, it's important to be a good doggie guest. Many hotels and motels have opened their accommodations to dog owners, and now it's up to dog owners to keep dogs welcome. Being a good doggie guest means keeping your dog on leash and under control. Don't let your dog run wild down hotel hallways. Be courteous and mindful of other guests. Make sure that you've worked on basic manners and obedience with your dog before traveling

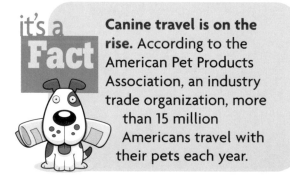

it's a Fact

Canine travel is on the rise. According to the American Pet Products Association, an industry trade organization, more than 15 million Americans travel with their pets each year.

with him. Don't leave a dog who is going to bark incessantly alone in a room for most of the night. In fact, most hotels ask that your dog be crated when you are not in the room with him, which is another excellent reason to cratetrain your Cavalier as a puppy. Lastly, pick up your dog's waste. Don't leave surprises around the outside of your accommodations for other unsuspecting guests to step in. If you clean up after your dog and he is well schooled in basic obedience and manners, you are sure to be asked to return to your favorite destination spot.

When you can't travel with your Cavalier, you'll need to make arrangements for him to be properly looked after in your absence. Today, there are many options for dog owners who need someone to care for their dogs in certain circumstances. While many people think of boarding their dogs as something to do when away on vacation, many others use the services of doggie day-care facilities, dropping their dogs off to spend the day while they are at work. Many of these facilities offer both long-term and daily care. Many go beyond just boarding and cater to

When traveling, be sure to make plenty of rest stops so your Cav can stretch her legs. Keep her on a leash, though.

all sorts of needs, with on-site grooming, veterinary care, training classes and even webcams where owners can log on to the internet and check out what their dogs are up to. Most dogs enjoy the activity and time spent with other dogs.

Before you need to use such a service, check out the ones in your area. Make visits to see the facilities, meet the staff, discuss fees and available services and see whether this is a place where you think your dog will be happy. It is best to do your research in advance so that you're not stuck at the last minute, forced into making a rushed decision without knowing whether the kennel you've chosen meets your standards. You can also check with your vet's office to see whether they offer boarding for clients or can recommend a good kennel in the area.

The kennel will need to see proof of your dog's health records and vaccinations so as not to spread illness from dog to dog. Your dog also will need proper identification. Owners usually experience some separation anxiety the first time they have to leave their dogs in someone else's care, so it's reassuring to know that the kennel you choose is run by experienced, caring, true dog people.

PET SITTERS

An alternative to the traditional boarding kennel is a pet sitter, someone who comes to your house to take care of your dog. This way your Cav can stay in his home where he's comfortable. Staying in a familiar environment can cut down on the stress your dog experiences when you're away. You'll have the peace of mind of knowing that your lovable pooch is at home being cared for and receiving one-on-one attention.

Pet sitters don't just make sure the dogs have food and water. They'll also walk the dogs, play with them and make sure they get veterinary attention, if needed. Also, pet sitters typically offer additional services, such as bringing in mail and newspapers, watering plants, turning lights on and off, and providing homes with a lived-in appearance to deter crime. However, like any other service, you should do your research. Just because people call themselves pet sitters doesn't necessarily mean they are qualified to do the job.

To find a reliable pet sitter, start by asking for recommendations from friends, neighbors, your veterinarian or a dog trainer. You can also contact the National Association of Professional Pet Sitters or Pet Sitters International for a referral. Both organizations offer pet-sitter accreditation to those who demonstrate professional experience, complete pet-care-related home study courses, attend professional conferences and abide by a code of ethics set by the organizations.

Once you have a few prospects, it's time for some important interview questions either over the phone or in person. Ask your prospective pet sitter the following:

- Can you provide written proof of commercial liability insurance (to cover accidents and negligence), and are you bonded (to protect against theft by a pet sitter or his employees)?
- What training have you received?
- Will you record notes about my pet, such as his likes, dislikes, fears, habits, medical conditions, medications and routines?
- Are you associated with a veterinarian who can provide emergency services?
- What will happen if you have car trouble or become ill? Do you have a backup?
- Do you have a written service contract spelling out services and fees?
- If you provide live-in services, what are the specific times you agree to be with the pet? Is this detailed in the contract?

- Can you provide phone numbers of other clients who have agreed to serve as references?

If you're happy with all the answers you get, it's still important to have the pet sitter visit your house and meet your dog. It's a good idea to see how the pet sitter and your Cavalier interact with each other and to see if the pet sitter truly seems comfortable with your dog. When using a pet sitter for the first time, you may want to plan a very short trip away for just one or two nights. This way you can see how everything goes and decide if you are happy with the sitter's service before you go for a longer trip farther away.

Whether your Cavalier is traveling with you or staying at home the key is to plan ahead and make sure that your four-legged friend has been properly socialized, has all his vaccinations, is crate trained and knows some basic obedience. This will ensure that your Cavalier is ready to travel or be easily cared for in your absence.

ID FOR YOUR DOG

You love your Cavalier and want to keep him safe. Of course, you take every precaution to prevent his escaping from the yard or becoming lost or stolen. You have a sturdy high fence, and you always keep your dog on leash when out and about in public places. If your dog is not properly identified, however, you are overlooking a major aspect of his safety. We hope to never be in a situation where our dogs are missing, but we should practice prevention in the unfortunate case that it happens. Identification greatly increases the chances of your dog being returned to you.

There are several ways to identify your Cav. First, the traditional dog tag should be a staple in your pet's wardrobe, attached to his collar. Tags can be made of sturdy plastic and various metals, and they should include your contact information so that a person who finds the dog can get in touch with you right away to arrange his return. Many people today enjoy the wide range of decorative tags available, so have fun and create a tag to match your dog's personality. Of course, it's important that the tag stays on the collar, so have a secure ring attachment; you also can consider the type of tag that slides right onto the collar.

One precaution to keep in mind is that your Cavalier shouldn't be left in a crate unattended with a collar on. There's a chance that the collar could get caught on some part of the crate and cause an injury.

In addition to the ID tag, which every dog should wear even if identified by another method, two other forms of identification have become popular: microchipping and tattooing. In microchipping, a tiny scannable chip is painlessly inserted under the dog's skin. The number is registered to you so that, if your lost dog turns up at a clinic or shelter, the chip can be scanned to retrieve your contact information. The advantage of the microchip is that it is a permanent form of ID, but there are some factors to consider. Several different companies make microchips, and not all are compatible with each others' scanning devices. It's best to find a company with a universal microchip that can be read by scanners made by other companies as well. It won't do any good to have the dog chipped if the information can't be retrieved. Also, not every humane society, shelter and clinic is equipped with a scanner, although more and more facilities are equipping themselves. In fact, many shelters microchip dogs that they adopt out to new homes.

In the United States, there are several major microchip manufacturers, as well as a few databases. Because the microchip is not visible to the eye, the dog must wear a tag that states that he is microchipped so that whoever picks him up will know to have him scanned. He also should have a tag with contact information in case his chip cannot be read. Humane societies and veterinary clinics offer this service, which is usually very affordable. When your dog is microchipped, you will receive information about adding your dog to the microchip company's database. It is very important to always keep your contact information up to date with the company. If you move or change your phone number, make sure to contact the microchip company with your new information.

Although it's less popular than microchipping, tattooing is another permanent method of canine identification. Most vets perform this service, and there are also clinics that perform dog tattooing. This is an affordable procedure and one that won't cause much discomfort for your Cavalier. It's best to put the tattoo in a visible area, such as the ear, to deter theft. It is sad to say that there are cases of dogs being stolen and sold to research laboratories, but such laboratories won't accept tattooed dogs.

To ensure that the tattoo is effective in aiding your dog's return to you, the tattoo number must be registered with a national organization. That way, when someone finds a tattooed dog, a phone call to the registry will quickly match the dog with his owner.

Many hotels today cater to people who travel with their pets.

INDEX

Academy of Veterinary
    Homeopathy 163
Adoption 39
Agility Trials 138
Aging,
    signs 151
Airborne Allergies 79
Alansmere Aquarius (first
    CKCS Best in Show at
    Crufts) 26
Alpha Dog 50
American
    Animal Hospital
    Association 163
American Cavalier
    King Charles
    Spaniel Club 30, 163
American Dog Owners
    Association 163
American Holistic
    Veterinary Medical
    Association 164
American
    Kennel Club 28, 164
American
    Veterinary Medical
    Association 164
Anal Glands 77
Association of
    Pet Dog Trainers 164
Asymptomatic
    Thrombocytopenia 80
Autoimmune Illness 79
Ayer, Deborah 35
Barking 123, 127
    "idiot" (idiopathic) 128
Basic Cues 112
    come 118
    down 116
    heel 120
    sit 114
    stay 116
Bedding 54

Bielakiewicz,
    Gerilyn J. 115
Blenheim 5, 8
Bowls,
    food and water 52
Breed,
    registration
    application 36
    rescue 39
    standard 4
Breeder
    Sales Contract 36
British Dogs 23
Brown, Cathy 63
Burkley, Pam 107
Cancer 152
Canine Performance
    Events 164
Cataracts 78
Cavalier King
    Charles Spaniel
    Club–USA 28, 36
Ch. Ravenrush Dizzie
    Gillespie (first CKCS
    AKC Best in Show) 28
Chambers,
    Jonathan N. 83
Characteristics,
    coloring 8, 21
    physical 8, 21
Chewing 130, 132
Cognitive
    Dysfunction 152
Cold Symptoms 76
Collars 56
Coprophagia 130
Crates 52
    pads 54
    -training 62
Crufts Dog Show 26
Dalziel, Hugh 23
DellaMaggiore, Dario 15
Delta Society 164

Dental Care 106
    plaque 99
    tartar 99
Dewclaws 108
Diarrhea 77
Digging 126
Discipline 123
Dog,
    shows 148
    sports 137
Dog Scouts
    of America 164
Dry Eye 78
Ear Care 104
Eye Care 104
Eldridge, Roswell 24
English Toy Spaniel 24
Enzymatic Cleaner 64
Escoe, Adrienne 18
Euthanasia 157
Exercise 137
External Parasites 79
Family Introduction 46
First Aid,
    cuts and scrapes 76
Fleas 80
    -control 109
Flyball 148
Food 87
    active-dog formula 94
    adult-formula 92
    bowls 52
    dry 88, 92
    puppy-formula 88
    semimoist 88
    senior-dog formula 94
    snacks 97
    treats 97
    trigger ingredients 95
    wet 88
Food–related
    Problems 128
Gates 111

Grieving 159
Grooming 99
  bathing 99
  brushing 99
  ear cleaning 104
  nail clipping 99
  needs 21
  routine 99
  tail docking 108
Hassig, Kris 93
Health,
  guarantee 36
  record 36
Healthy Puppy Signs 42
Heartworm 84
Hetts, Suzanne 133
Hill, Barbara 89
Hip Dysplasia 79
Home Safety 56
Hookworms 82
Housetraining 59
  adult dogs 60
  schedule 69
  tips 66
Intelligence 16, 112
Interaction,
  with cats 46, 124
  with children 14, 21
  with other pets 14, 21
Internal Parasites 82
Kennel Club
  (England) 26
King Charles I 4, 24
King Charles II 23, 24
King Charles
  Spaniel (English) 24
King James II 24
Lap Dog 51
Leashes 56, 111
Macrothrombocytosis 80
Mary Queen of Scots 23
Merry Monarch, The 24
Mites 82

Mitral Valve Disease 78
Moro, Antonio 23
Musical Freestyle 149
Nash,
  Joanne 25, 85, 143
Neuter 42
Nipping 132
Obedience Trials 144
Origin 21, 23
Outside Potty Area 60
Patellar Luxation
  (slipped kneecap) 74
Pedigree 36
Performance
  Activities 137
Personality 7, 12, 21
Pet Identification 172
Pet Sitting 170
Pet Sitters
  International 165
Pet travel,
  airline 167
  car 166
  dog-friendly
    destinations 168
Phillip of Spain 23
Poison Ingestion 77
Potty Accidents 64
Preventive Health 82
Puppy
  kindergarten 114
  visitation 34
  -proofing 50
Queen Mary I 23
Rally 146
Roundworms 82
Sally Lyons Brown 28
Santo, Kathy 117
Selection,
  breeder 34
  puppy 34
  veterinarian 71
  trainer 112

Senior dogs 151
  care 154
  common ailments 152
Separation Anxiety 124
Show Dogs 148
Slicker Brush 106
Socialization 38
Solomon, Christine 43
Spay 42
Syringomyelia 78
Tapeworms 84
Therapy Dogs
  International 165
Threadworms 84
Ticks 80
Toys 54
  homemade 52
Tracking 142
Training 111
  clicker 112
  positive
    reinforcement 111
  tools 111
United Kennel Club 165
United States
  Dog Agility
  Association 165
Unwanted Jumping 133
Vaccination Schedule 74
Vaccines 74
Van Dyck, Anthony 157
Vomiting 77
Walker, Mostyn 26
Water,
  bowls 52
  intake 96
Weight Problems 152
Whining 135
Whipworms 84
Wilson,
  Barbara Garnett 29
Wolff, Caryl 67
Wood, Deborah 53

INDEX

CAVALIER KING CHARLES SPANIEL, a Smart Owner's Guide®
part of the Kennel Club Books® Interactive Series®

JOIN
**Club
Cav™**
TODAY!

LIBRARY OF CONGRESS CATALOGING-IN-PUBLICATION DATA

Cavalier King Charles spaniel.
     p. cm. — (A smart owner's guide)
Includes bibliographical references and index.
ISBN 978-1-59378-753-0 (alk. paper)
1. Cavalier King Charles spaniel. I. Kennel Club Books.
SF429.C36C38 2011
636.752′4—dc22

                     2010032951